Teachers
Bringing Out the

Best

in Teachers

To educational leaders—both teachers and administrators—who nurture a natural and powerful form of teacher growth: peer consultation

Teachers
Bringing Out the

Best
in Teachers

A Guide to
Peer Consultation
for Administrators and Teachers

Jo Blase
Joseph J. Blase
FOREWORD BY Edith Rusch

CORWIN PRESS
A SAGE Publications Company
Thousand Oaks, California

For information:

Corwin Press
A Sage Publications Company
2455 Teller Road
Thousand Oaks, California 91320
www.corwinpress.com

Sage Publications Ltd.
1 Oliver's Yard
55 City Road
London EC1Y 1SP
United Kingdom

Sage Publications India Pvt. Ltd.
B-42, Panchsheel Enclave
Post Box 4109
New Delhi 110 017 India

Printed in the United States of America on acid-free paper

Library of Congress Cataloging-in-Publication Data

Blase, Jo Roberts.
Teachers bringing out the best in teachers : a guide to peer consultation for administrators and teachers / Jo Blase, Joseph J. Blase.
    p. cm.
Includes bibliographical references and index.
ISBN 1-4129-2595-9 (cloth) — ISBN 1-4129-2596-7 (pbk.)
   1. Teaching—Vocational guidance—United States. 2. Teachers—Professional relationships—United States. 3. Teacher-principal relationships—United States. I. Blase, Joseph. II. Title.
LB1775.2.B58 2006
371.10023—dc22   2006004641

06 07 08 09 10   10 9 8 7 6 5 4 3 2 1

Acquisitions editor:	Elizabeth Brenkus
Editorial assistant:	Desirée Enayati
Production editor:	Sanford Robinson
Copy editor:	Heather Moore
Typesetter:	C&M Digitals (P) Ltd.
Indexer:	Molly Hall
Cover designer:	Michael Dubowe

Contents

Foreword

Several years ago, I introduced a new course into our leadership preparation program titled Leading the Learner Centered School. The content was predicated on the notion that teachers' primary focus is on learners and learning. In my view, a deep understanding of that precept would assist aspiring school leaders to become more effective instructional leaders. A major assignment for students in this class was to partner with a learner of any age and spend the semester teaching each other about learning. The assignment culminated with a *learning fair* where each member of the class demonstrated the insights gained from the assigned consultation. I have fond memories of a music teacher bringing his partners—a quartet of sophomores who had taught him how capable they were at self-organizing—to compose unique music. Their performance in our class was a unique culmination to our busy semester. Some students invited teaching partners and shared an action research process related to instructional decisions. Not everyone *displayed* live partners, but each demonstration paralleled the remarkable findings of the book you find in your hands—when individuals spend time together talking about learning, instruction changes, learners engage, and achievement improves. That is the core message of Jo and Joe Blase in *Teachers Bringing Out the Best in Teachers*.

This book ought to be required reading for every aspiring and practicing principal because it truly represents an enlightened conversation about instructional leadership. In this age of NCLB (No Child Left Behind), educational administrators at all levels of schooling are charged with being instructional leaders, yet the actual implementation of that concept remains a pretty contested notion. Some school administrators lead instruction through close supervision of highly prescribed classroom behaviors. Others lead by joining the "Idea of the Month Club," overwhelming teachers with new approaches, new resources, and countless projects. Still others spend precious dollars on *gurus* who offer the latest fix for raising test scores. Study after study reports minimal gains in achievement from any of these approaches.

The treasure that Jo and Joe Blase offer to us in *Teachers Bringing Out the Best in Teachers* is that instructional leadership may be a far simpler concept than usually portrayed. This book is filled with voices of teachers who provide rich descriptions of their informal talk, detailing how a peer consultation process leads to improved instruction, better classroom management, and a deeper understanding of individual learners. As the authors note, "Teaching may be one of the few professions in which practitioners generously and passionately help colleagues and do this in spite of numerous barriers" (Chapter 5, p. 81). Principals have the power to remove the barriers, either structural, organizational, or human. If we listen carefully to and reflect on the words of these peer consultants in our midst, the role of an instructional leader becomes crystal clear. Effective instructional leaders do one thing: organize an environment that supports teacher conversation about learning.

The Blases' research makes visible the link between research-based knowledge and craft knowledge. Frequently, educators are cognizant of the research that touts positive learning outcomes of an innovative instructional approach. However, the actual implementation of the practice, the day-to-day organizing actions, may not be revealed in the research. Adult learners expect to master an idea very quickly; and if the experience of a new approach is messy for too long, they will give up on the practice despite research findings. The teacher voices in this book provide vivid descriptions of critical analyses and reflective work about daily practice in efforts to master new approaches. As they consult with peers, their craft knowledge clearly supports the adult *learning curve*.

This book challenges one other long-held assumption about teaching: that it is an isolated task. As I read the words of the many teachers in this study, I realized that despite the deep isolation of our organizational structures, teachers find multiple points of contact that break the isolation to hone their craft. In many cases, their informal talk fosters awareness of how easily classrooms become teacher centered rather than learner centered. One study participant noted how "self-examination made me realize that. The student's needs should come first" (Chapter 3, p. 56).

Clearly, I appreciate this new work by authors who have committed their professional lives to improving the experience of educating in our schools. I also am aware that many school leaders, who are committed to improving instruction, still struggle with the *how* of the work and resort to formal supervision and evaluation as a primary tool. This book provides more than a roadmap for the work of an instructional leader; the book itself is the journey. I encourage principals and teachers to use this book as a vehicle to foster faculty learning about learning. Each chapter contains powerful questions and implications for practice, as well as additional references that extend the topics. The most effective instructional leadership comes from principals who recognize and legitimize the natural tendency among educators to collaborate about learning. Used in this manner, school leaders may locate a new set of voices with rich data that will only improve our learner outcomes.

—Edith Rusch
Associate Professor, University of Las Vegas

Preface

[T]he most reliable, useful, proximate, and professional help [for teachers] resides under the roof of the schoolhouse with the teaching staff itself.

—Barth, 2001, p. 445

This book is written for classroom teachers, lead teachers, teachers on special assignment, department chairpersons, principals, assistant principals, professional learning coordinators, and staff developers who want to promote teacher collegiality and school improvement by enabling teachers to collaborate on instructional matters. Uniquely, this book is not about formal professional development opportunities; rather, it is about naturally occurring, informal, spontaneous, timely, and relevant collaboration among teachers, that is, *peer consultation*. Peer consultation refers to two or more teachers engaging in dialogue about the idiosyncratic teaching context and individual teachers' concerns. The focus of peer consultation is usually selected by the teacher who needs help, and peer consultants do not necessarily have expertise specific to a given teacher's work. Thus, peer consultants are nonthreatening partners who facilitate a teacher's reflection on teaching-learning issues, assessment of progress, and instructional improvement. The peer consultant is the unnoticed *other* who helps teachers blend scientific and craft knowledge in the complex, challenging, and often messy world of teaching and learning.

Teachers Bringing Out the Best in Teachers is based on a study of several hundred teachers from public elementary, middle, and high schools located in the southeastern United States. We asked our research participants to describe, in detail, the actions of other teachers that directly or indirectly helped them teach more effectively. We also asked them to discuss the personal and professional effects (i.e., effects on thinking, teaching, and feelings) of such teacher–teacher interaction. This book presents teachers' perspectives on peer consultation.

Heretofore, the world of peer consultation has been relatively invisible. It exists outside the formal practice of instructional supervision by a principal (which sadly and all too often disintegrates into control and bureaucratic snooping), outside the formal work of lead teachers and teacher leaders (which also often disintegrates into a *neither-teacher-nor-principal* role for teacher leaders and alienates other teachers), and outside the world of emergent teacher leadership (i.e., career lattices, collaborative leadership, and constructivist leadership). Peer consultation, we found, capitalizes on teacher expertise and is an effective vehicle for strengthening trust and respect among teachers, creating a positive learning environment for teachers as learners, and creating positive impacts on instruction. It results in teacher growth, confidence, and school improvement. Indeed, the peer consultant appears to be the ultimate coach for teachers, and peer consultation may well be the last frontier in teacher learning and development. We found that peer consultation is powerful in the subtle but certain way that it can develop instructional expertise and build a culture of shared effort and critical self-reflection among teachers.

This book illuminates basic elements of effective peer consultation and describes how it supports both teacher and student learning. The centerpiece of this book is the result of our study of teachers' perspectives of peer consultation, including countless excerpts from our database that illustrate select ideas. Specifically, we present descriptions of what peer consultants actually do that leads to impacts such as improved teacher confidence and motivation, enhanced mutual respect, and reflective instructional behavior. In each chapter we present relevant concepts and strategies from the literature that will help educators think through their approach to peer consultation. We also synthesize and present extant empirical, conceptual, and theoretical literature in detailed figures and tables throughout the book. Finally, we include relevant questions, suggestions, or a discussion of implications for practice in each chapter. Taken together, our database, the literature, and our model of peer con sultation provide an approach to peer consultation based on trust, collaboration, reflection, and collaborative inquiry.

What does peer consultation look like in practice? What effects does it have on teachers, teaching, and classroom management? Chapter 1 reviews the three major sources of teacher help: principals as instructional supervisors, lead teachers, and peer consultants. A brief overview of our major findings about peer consultation and a host of figures that summarize relevant literature are also included. Peer consultation skill #1, building healthy relationships by communicating, caring, and building trust is discussed in Chapter 2. Chapters 3, 4, 5, and 6 focus on the critical skills used by peer consultants as they help teachers, including peer consultation skill #2, using the five guiding principles for structuring learning principles; peer consultation skill #3, planning for organizing and learning; peer consultation skill #4, showing and sharing; and peer consultation skill #5, guiding for classroom management, respectively. Chapter 7, the final chapter, discusses some of the major conclusions of our study, our expanded model of academic leadership, and the relationship between peer consultation and the development of a professional learning community in schools. Research methods are found in the resource section at the end of the book.

Because of increasing teacher shortages and fiscal challenges, American schools will be increasingly staffed by alternatively certified (and likely less able) teachers at a time when such schools cannot afford more administrators to provide instructional leadership. Fortunately, extra instructional help can be found in those talented and high-performing teachers who are naturally drawn to assist their peers' development in timely and spontaneous ways. Join us now to peer in on our peers to find them doing what comes naturally: lending a hand to colleagues engaged in the vital mission of our schools—educating our youth.

Acknowledgments

Corwin Press gratefully acknowledges the contributions of the following individuals:

Edith Rusch, Associate Professor
Department of Educational Leadership
University of Nevada Las Vegas
Las Vegas, NV

Gwen Gross
Superintendent of Schools
Manhattan Beach Unified School District
Manhattan Beach, CA

Matt Jennings, Assistant Superintendent
Berkeley Heights Public Schools
Berkeley Heights, NJ

Shelby Cosner, Assistant Professor
Policy Studies, College of Education
University of Illinois at Chicago
Chicago, IL

About the Authors

 **Jo Blase** is a professor of educational leadership and codirector of ATLAS, the Alliance for Teaching, Leadership, and School Improvement, at the University of Georgia as well as a former public school teacher, high school and middle school principal, and director of staff development. She received a Ph.D. in educational administration, curriculum, and supervision in 1983 from the University of Colorado at Boulder. Through work with the Beginning Principal Study National Research Team, the Georgia League of Professional Schools, and public and private school educators with whom she consults throughout the United States, she has pursued her interest in preparation for and entry to educational and instructional leadership as it relates to supervisory discourse.

Blase has been the winner of the WG Walker 2000 Award for Excellence for her coauthored article published in the *Journal of Educational Administration*, the 1997 University of Georgia College of Education Teacher Educator Award, and the 1983 American Association of School Administrators Outstanding Research Award. Her recent publications include articles in the *Journal of Staff Development*, the *Journal of Curriculum and Supervision*, *Educational Administration Quarterly*, and *The Alberta Journal of Educational Research* as well as the books *Empowering Teachers: What Successful Principals Do* (with Joseph Blase; Corwin Press, 1994, 2001), *Democratic Principals in Action: Eight Pioneers* (with Joseph Blase, Gary Anderson, and Sherry Dungan; Corwin Press, 1995), *The Fire is Back: Principals Sharing School Governance* (with Joseph Blase; Corwin Press, 1997), *Handbook of Instructional Leadership* (with Joseph Blase; Corwin Press, 1998, 2004), and *Breaking the Silence: Overcoming the Problem of Principal Mistreatment of Teachers* (Corwin Press, 2002). She has authored chapters on becoming a principal, school renewal, supervision, and organizational development. In addition, she conducts research on supervisory discourse among physicians as medical educators.

 **Joseph Blase** is a professor of educational leadership and codirector of ATLAS, the Alliance for Teaching, Leadership, and School Improvement, in the College of Education at the University of Georgia. Since receiving his Ph.D. in 1980 from Syracuse University, his research has focused on understanding the work lives of teachers. He has published many studies in the areas of teacher stress, relationships between teachers' personal and professional lives, teacher socialization, and principal-teacher relationships. His work concentrating on school-level micropolitics received the 1988 Davis Memorial Award given by the University Council for Educational Administration, and his coauthored article published in the *Journal of Educational Administration* won the WG Walker 2000 Award for Excellence. Blase edited *The Politics of Life in Schools: Power, Conflict, and Cooperation* (winner of the 1994 Critic's Choice Award sponsored by the American Education Studies Association; Sage, 1991); coauthored with Peggy Kirby, *Bringing Out the Best in Teachers* Corwin Press, 1994, 2000); coauthored with Jo Blase, Gary Anderson, and Sherry Dungan, *Democratic Principals in Action: Eight Pioneers* (Corwin Press, 1995); coauthored with Gary Anderson, *The Micropolitics of Educational Leadership* (Teachers College Press, 1995); and coauthored with Jo Blase, *Empowering Teachers* (1994, 2001), *The Fire is Back: Principals Sharing School Governance* (Corwin Press, 1997), *Handbook of Instructional Leadership* (1998, 2004), and *Breaking the Silence: Overcoming the Problem of Principal Mistreatment of Teachers* (2003). His numerous articles appear in journals such as the *American Education Research Journal* and *Educational Administration Quarterly*; and his chapters appear in international handbooks of research on change and teaching.

1

Teachers Helping Teachers: The Case for Peer Consultation

The nonparticipation of teachers in decisions that bear directly on their daily work environment leads both to a decline in self-esteem and to strong feelings of external control by others. Over time, these effects take their toll, manifesting themselves first in terms of job stress and ultimately in perceptions of diminished personal accomplishment.

—Byrne, 1994, p. 665

Enormous risks and frequent costs are associated with observation, communication, mutual visibility, sharing knowledge, and talking openly about the work teachers do. Collegiality requires that everyone be willing to give up something without knowing in advance just what that may be. But the risks and costs of interdependence are nothing next to the risks and costs of sustaining a climate of emotional toxicity, of working in isolation.

—Barth, 1990, p. 31

INTRODUCTION

In recent years, many American school administrators have realized that the work of school improvement is best accomplished when shared with teachers. These educational leaders have wisely empowered teachers to collaborate in a variety of joint endeavors, including peer coaching, mentoring, collegial investigations using action research, explorations into instructional challenges, study teams, and problem solving. Clearly, promoting teacher collegiality has been one leadership approach that has yielded answers to teaching and learning problems, enabling teachers to effectively work together to develop instructional alternatives and processes that lead to the development of a community of learners engaged in professional service to children.

Unfortunately, collaborative approaches to educators' work have often been associated with confusion about teachers' professional role definitions, human and financial costs, and lack of time for professional talk. And, teachers' work experience continues to be predominantly an individual and isolated practice of teaching. In spite of such difficulties, many teachers not otherwise engaged in peer coaching, mentoring, or similar formal programs appear to have gained substantial knowledge and support from *informal peer consultation* with colleagues and have skillfully applied this knowledge to their daily classroom work with students. Interestingly, however, *there are no published comprehensive descriptions of the content, process, and context of spontaneous, naturally occurring peer consultation among teachers.* Therefore, we initiated a study to illuminate this important but heretofore hidden (at least in terms of the research literature) phenomenon.

The purpose of this book is to describe the results of our study of peer consultation. Derived directly from our study data, our concept of peer consultation refers to teacher-to-teacher consultation; specifically, it involves spontaneous, timely, and unstructured patterns of behavior of teachers helping teachers. This, we discovered, is a world of informal and yet profound discovery, career-changing encounters, and mutual spiritual growth between and among teachers. It is a world in which teachers intuitively reach out to each other to talk about and reflect on their work, to make use of their knowledge, to collectively plan and organize for teaching, to share with and show each other valuable resources, and to guide each other in managing the complexities of student learning and behavior. In addition, although in many cases the practical implications of our findings are obvious, we include questions and actionable steps professional educators should consider when implementing efforts to develop or improve peer consultation in their school. As the reader will see at the end of this chapter, five primary skills comprise peer consultation; and each is explicated in succeeding chapters replete with teacher quotes, examples, and suggestions.

We introduce our journey into this hidden world of peer consultation with a look at what we know about teacher learning, followed by brief descriptions of three primary sources of teacher-to-teacher assistance for learning discussed in the professional literature:

1. Administrators who engage in instructional supervision

2. Lead teachers who fulfill formal and/or emergent roles in assisting teachers

3. Teachers as peer consultants who spontaneously assist their colleagues

In addition, we present our Peer Consultation Model (PCM)—consisting of five key elements—derived directly from the study that serves as the basis for this book. Finally, we briefly describe the research method and procedures used to conduct the study that is the basis of this book, and we highlight some of our most important findings about peer consultation.

HOW TEACHERS LEARN TO TEACH

Although it is a widely accepted premise that each teacher is unique, the conceptual work necessary to differentiate programs for individual teachers' professional growth is unavailable (Burden, 1990). Nevertheless, extant knowledge about individual development characteristics and phases of adult life informs our efforts to adapt teachers' learning opportunities to their needs; for example, research has focused on adults' cognitive development (Sprinthall & Thies-Sprinthall, 1980), developmental ages and cycles (Erikson, 1959; Gould, 1972), and developmental stages (including cognitive, moral, ego, conceptual, ethical, and interpersonal development; e.g., Piaget, 1963; Kohlberg, 1969). This research has also illuminated teachers' developmental concerns (Fuller & Brown, 1975) and patterns of career development (Gregorc, 1979). Furthermore, it is generally accepted that principles of adult learning should be considered in creating opportunities for teacher growth. Learning is life centered and based on adult interests and prior experience; learning is self-directed and includes a process of inquiry with others; and individual differences, which increase with age, are addressed (see Knowles, 1978).

In light of these principles, what defines the best form of professional development for teachers? The most concise statement of standards for teachers' professional development, drawn from research on staff and teacher development and student learning, is the National Staff Development Council's 12 Standards (National Staff Development Council [NSDC], 2001). These standards address the context, process, and content of staff development and teacher learning:

1. Teachers form learning communities whose goals match those of the school and district.

2. Leaders provide guidance for continuous school improvement.

3. Resources for adult learning and collaboration are provided for professional development programs.

4. Professional development programs are data based.

5. Assessment of student learning is continuous.

6. Professional development programs are research based.

7. Professional development programs match school goals.

8. Professional development programs adhere to adult learning principles.

9. Professional development programs enable teacher collaboration.

10. Professional development programs reflect high expectations for all students.

11. Professional development programs deepen teachers' content knowledge, teaching strategies, and assessment ability.

12. Professional development programs encourage family involvement.

Given what we know about professional development—including knowledge of teacher development, adult learning, staff development, and related impacts on student learning—we posit that any *one* of the three sources of teacher assistance described in the table that follows is inadequate for effective teacher growth and that the enhancement of *peer consultation* (the third source of teacher assistance) with its inherent timeliness, individualization, contextualization, and use of teacher expertise is vital. The remaining chapters of this book include a deep exploration into this third source of teacher assistance, peer consultation.

Three Sources of Teacher Assistance

1. Principals

2. Lead Teachers

3. Peer Consultants

THE FIRST SOURCE OF TEACHER HELP: PRINCIPALS AS INSTRUCTIONAL SUPERVISORS

Throughout the last 150 years, instructional supervision of teachers by principals has been viewed in both dark side (negative) and bright side (positive) terms, particularly with regard to practice. On the dark side, instructional supervision has been referred to as *inspection, snooper-vision,* and a *nonevent* (Figure 1.1). Guthrie and Willower (1973) concluded that the ritual (of supervision, the sporadic observation of teaching for the purpose of rating general competence) is a harmless and often useless exercise, a *ceremonial congratulation.* At its worst, principals' instructional supervision has been linked to maintaining excessive control over teachers, interrupting teaching, abandoning teachers, and destructively criticizing teachers (Figure 1.2) (Blase & Blase, 2004a).

On the bright side, theoretically at least, instructional supervision has been oriented to collaboration between teachers and supervisors and the development of teacher reflection on practice; in fact, it has been described as a *collegial and transformational event* (Blase & Blase, 2001). Figure 1.3 describes the bright side of instructional supervision by principals, as reported in our earlier study (Blase & Blase, 2001). In that study more than 800 teachers across the United States described the basic elements of effective instructional supervision (i.e., instructional leadership) and its dramatic effects on teaching and student learning. From these data we developed a holistic model—the TiGeR model of principals' instructional supervision—based on three powerful principal strategies: *T*alking with teachers, promoting teachers' professional *G*rowth, and fostering teacher *R*eflection. The specific principle behaviors associated with these strategies include, for example, building trust, applying principles of adult growth and development, and developing teachers' reflection skills.

We found that these strategies contributed to the development of a school culture of collaboration, equality, inquiry, and the lifelong study of teaching and learning. Positive impacts on teacher reflection, creativity, innovation, experimentation, and risk taking as well as impacts on teachers' self-esteem, motivation, and confidence were also evident. Clearly, a supervisory approach such as the TiGeR model enables a principal to be a facilitator of teacher growth rather than an inspector of teacher competence (Poole, 1995), a colleague in discussing alternatives rather than directives or criticisms (Blase & Blase, 2001), and a developer of collaborative inquiry rather than a unilateral purveyor of standards (Reitzug, 1997).

In recent years, approaches to instructional supervision that increase teacher control and responsibility for professional growth and instructional improvement, such as collegial supervision, individually planned professional development, standards-based supervision, reflective supervision, and collegial supervision have gained acceptance among principals and teachers (Glickman, Gordon, & Ross-Gordon, 2004; Sullivan & Glanz, 2004). The collegial supervision approach includes a *collegial*—not hierarchical—relationship between teachers and supervisors; the *involvement* of teachers in peer supervision and growth; a *focus on growth,* not compliance; teacher *collaboration;* and ongoing *reflective inquiry* by teachers (Gordon, 1997). In essence, collegial supervision is status free, and the underlying spirit is one of expansion and alternatives rather than directives or criticisms; it is a type of peer collaboration in which a community of teacher learners performs professional and moral services to students.

Figure 1.1   The Instructional Supervision Legacy: Control or Collaboration?

In 1993 Cogan, Anderson, and Krajewski classified [principals'] supervision approaches that have appeared in the professional literature between 1850 and 1990:

1. Scientific management
2. Democratic interaction approach
3. Cooperative supervision
4. Supervision as curriculum development
5. Clinical supervision
6. Group dynamics and peer emphasis
7. Coaching and instructional supervision

Krajewski (1996) described contemporary approaches to supervision as *almost collaborative*— almost, but not truly collaborative—the author suggests, because power differentials still exist between principals and teachers, given the principals' evaluation responsibilities (power to judge) and change-agent role. Krajewski predicts that by the year 2015 supervision will consist of *structured options* (i.e., based on some standards and expectations but also based on teachers' individual needs and goals, much like a student's individual educational plan [IEP]).

However, the array of approaches to supervision noted previously indicates that substantial disagreement about its essential nature has existed for more than 140 years. The *practice* of supervision is another matter. Despite the fact that many approaches to supervision are collaborative in nature, the practice of supervision has often been one of inspection, oversight, and judgment. Glanz (1995) concluded that today's supervision is nothing better than a "bureaucratic legacy of fault finding, inspectional supervision" and used terms like "snoopervision," "protective political behavior," and "a private cold war" (p. 107) to characterize the field. Sergiovanni (1992) referred to supervision as a "nonevent—a ritual they [supervisors and teachers] participate in according to well-established scripts without much consequence" (p. 203). More recently, Gordon (1997) stated, "In the present, control supervision [not collegiality and empowerment] still dominates professional practice" (p. 117).

We believe that although the idea of collegial supervision, in various forms, has existed for most of this century, advanced forms of collegiality are rarely found in practice. Indeed, democratic, cooperative, clinical, human resource–based, developmental, and transformational supervision, among others, have been widely advocated (Gordon, 1997) based on the principles of equality (not hierarchy), reflection, and growth (not compliance). For instance, Pajak (1993) noted that the goal (and, at times, the *emerging* practice) of supervision focuses on "helping teachers discover and construct professional knowledge and skills," in contrast to the established practice of "reinforcing specific prescribed teacher behavior and skills" (p. 318). He also noted that in much contemporary thinking, learning is viewed as contextual and complex, teaching is based on reflective judgment, and schools are seen as democratic teaching and learning communities.

Likewise, Schön's (1988) definition of instructional supervision emphasizes collegial supervision and specifically focuses on support, guidance, and encouragement of *reflective teaching*; and Glickman, Gordon, and Ross-Gordon (1995) described ideal supervision as a *collaborative* endeavor enacted in a supportive environment that leads to an all-school action plan. To promote collegial forms of supervision, McBride and Skau(1995) have proposed that practitioners develop a *supervisory platform*—a combination of supervisory beliefs and educational philosophy—which includes building *trust, empowering* teachers, and fostering *reflection*. They note, "The process of reflection, undertaken in an environment based on trust and seeking the empowerment of participants, constitutes a powerful potential for improved [supervisory and teaching] practice" (p. 277).

Relatedly, Reitzug and Cross (1993) have discussed an *inquiry-oriented* practice of supervision (*critical collaboration*) that encourages teacher voice and acknowledges the contextuality and complexity of teaching. Here, the principal's role is one of facilitating a teacher's thinking about practice. More broadly, Smyth (1997) has suggested that supervision advance a discursive, collaborative, and critical study of the *micropolitics of the classroom* interaction; relinquish its technocratic surveillance of teachers; and work toward a just and democratic world. He recommends giving teachers more, rather than less, control over their teaching.

SOURCE: Blase & Blase (2004a).

Figure 1.2   The Dark Side of Instructional Supervision: Effects of Selected
Principal Behaviors

Interrupting and abandoning teachers' classroom instruction results in:

Anger

Low motivation

Psychic pain

Feelings of abandonment

Loss of respect for principal

Poor performance

Criticizing teachers results in:

Anger

Low motivation

Damaged self-esteem

Fear

Confusion

Loss of respect and trust for principal

Appearing to comply, ignoring, avoiding the principal

Resistance and rebellion

Cautiousness

Excessive control of teachers' professional work results in:

Limited involvement in decision making
A false image of governance (if the principal's rhetoric and participatory structures suggest
collegiality)

A sense of being manipulated

Feeling abused (when the principal's rhetoric and practice contradict supposed
collegial governance structures)

SOURCE: Adapted from Blase & Blase (2004a).

Teacher Empowerment and School Improvement
Related to Principals' Supervision

Educational scholars have studied the effects of instructional supervision and instructional leadership on teacher empowerment and school improvement. To illustrate from a case study of instructional leadership,

Figure 1.3   The Bright Side of Instructional Supervision: How Principals Build
a Culture of Collaboration, Equality, and Lifelong Study of Teaching
and Learning

What characteristics (strategies, behaviors, attitudes, and goals) of school principals positively influence teachers' classroom instruction? What is it about supervisor–teacher interaction—with a specific emphasis on the talk that occurs in instructional supervisory conferences—that enables teachers to learn and apply such learnings to classroom instruction? How do principals develop a specialized form of teacher thinking—reflection—that arises from a teacher's questions about perplexing classroom experiences and leads to purposeful inquiry and problem resolution (Dewey, 1933)? Our study of positive forms of principals' instructional supervision vis-à-vis teachers sheds light on these and other critical questions thus far unaddressed by empirical research.

We found that in effective principal–teacher interaction about instruction, processes such as inquiry, reflection, exploration, and experimentation prevail; teachers build repertoires of flexible alternatives rather than collecting rigid teaching procedures and methods (Schön, 1987). Principals who are effective instructional supervisors develop a reflective, collaborative, problem-solving context for dialog about instruction by doing the following:

They *Talk* With Teachers

Build trust
Develop the group
Foster collaboration and collegiality
Support peer coaching
Observe in classrooms
Confer with teachers about teaching and learning
Empower teachers
Maintain visibility

They Promote Teachers' *Professional Growth*

Study literature and proven programs
Support practice of new skills, risk-taking, innovation, and creativity
Provide effective staff development programs
Apply principles of adult growth and development
Praise, support, and facilitate teachers' work
Provide resources and time
Give feedback and suggestions

They Foster Teacher *Reflection*

Develop teachers' reflection skills in order to construct professional
knowledge and develop sociopolitical insights
Model and develop teachers' critical study (action research) skill
Become inquiry oriented
Use data to question, evaluate, and critique teaching and learning
Extend autonomy to teachers

SOURCE: Adapted from Blase & Blase (2001).

Reitzug (1994) constructed a taxonomy of empowering principal behaviors that includes *support,* creating a supportive environment in which teachers can critique instruction; *facilitation,* stimulating critique of instruction by teachers; and *possibility,* giving teachers voice by publishing and acting on the results of critique.

This study was based on Prawat's (1991) framework for epistemological and political empowerment and consists of two categories—"conversations with self" and "conversations with settings" (p. 738)—wherein teachers develop inquiry skills, critical reflection skills, and even sociopolitical insights through alternative modes of professional interaction important to empowerment and school improvement. Reitzug demonstrated that principal leadership—providing meaningful staff development, modeling inquiry, asking questions, encouraging risk taking, requiring justification of practices, and critique by wandering around—led to greater levels of teacher empowerment and school improvement. These instructional supervision behaviors are similar to those we identified in research on empowering instructional principals (Blase & Blase, 1994, 1997; Blase, Blase, Anderson, & Dungan, 1995) and effective instructional leaders (Blase & Blase, 2004a).

THE SECOND SOURCE OF TEACHER HELP: LEAD TEACHERS AND THE MOVE AWAY FROM TOP-DOWN ADMINISTRATIVE CONTROL

The second wave of educational reform efforts in the United States was prompted by high-profile reports from The Carnegie Foundation (1986), the Holmes Group (1986), and the National Governors' Association (1986). All three reports recommended a move away from top-down approaches to school improvement; consequently, second wave–reform efforts initially emphasized the creation of career ladders for teachers and lead teacher positions, the second source of teacher help.

Formal Teacher Leadership

Early efforts to develop teachers' leadership roles emphasized creating *formal* positions such as lead teachers, instructional leaders, mentors, team leaders, and curriculum leaders in which teacher leaders were appointed by administrators and given formal authority to enact their roles ("appoint and anoint"; Smylie, 1995). This approach has been hindered by obstacles such as teachers' reluctance to consider themselves leaders and relate as equals to administrators; teachers' working norms including equality, autonomy, independence, and privacy; the nature of teachers' work, such as isolation and lack of time to collaborate; the ambiguity of the lead teacher's role; and the lack of training for the lead teacher's role (Pellicer & Anderson, 1995; Smylie & Brownlee-Conyers, 1992). *Generally, educational researchers have concluded that because of such obstacles, promoting teacher leadership through formal roles has been unsuccessful in achieving desired goals.* Formal mentoring programs, for example, have provided teachers with some emotional and technical support but have not prepared them for standards-based reform (Wang & Odell, 2002); and the strongest effects (although inconsistent) of teacher leadership have been on teacher leaders themselves, not their peers (e.g., reduced isolation, increased reflection, and intellectual stimulation) (York-Barr & Duke, 2004).

In addition, we now understand that life in schools is complex, dynamic, and profoundly political (Blase, 1991; Blase & Blase, 2002), as is the role of teacher leader. For example, teacher leaders are in a delicate relationship with school principals, a relationship often dominated by the principals' sense of accountability and control, as principals work to protect their authority and status. Additionally, to maintain relationships with other teachers, teacher leaders tend to avoid conflict and *play it safe*, rather than violate egalitarian cultural norms (Smylie & Denny, 1990). Indeed, formal teacher leadership is an organizational phenomenon rife with issues that complicate the teacher leader's work with teachers.

Informal (Emergent, Naturally Occurring) Teacher Leadership

Recently, educational scholars have called for a broader view of teacher leadership including *informal teacher leadership roles* (Darling-Hammond, Bullmaster, & Cobb, 1995; Odell, 1997; Smylie, 1995; Wasley, 1991). They have discussed the potential of less-structured, *emergent* forms of teacher leadership such as career lattices (Howey, 1988), collaborative leadership (Darling-Hammond et al., 1995), and constructivist leadership (Lambert et al., 1995); all forms of collaborative leadership based on experience, interest, expertise, and fluid and flexible relationships; they can be initiated by any teacher and become an integral part of the teacher's role and the school culture. From his study of teacher leadership, Odell (1997) concluded that when schools as a whole are "professionalized and better organized for teaching, teacher leaders will emerge as a matter of course in informally structured positions" (p. 121).

Emergent teacher leadership is best described by three concepts: career lattices, the Professional Development Schools approach, and constructivist leadership theory (Sabatini, 2002). First, in contrast to career ladders (a hierarchical approach in which teachers are given varying pay, status, and responsibility), the *career lattices* approach refers to a type of collaborative leadership in which all personnel in the educational enterprise work together. Career lattices empower teachers to engage in leadership opportunities, which vary by school needs and include, for example, planning and improving curriculum, developing instructional skills and strategies, and conducting action research. The career lattice approach allows for any and all teachers to be involved in roles that are fluid and flexible, and it implicitly acknowledges that teachers possess great expertise and knowledge that should be tapped to redesign and improve schools (Darling-Hammond et al., 1995).

Second, in *Professional Development Schools (PDSs)*, teacher leadership "is potentially more than a role; it is a *stance*, a mind-set, a way of being, acting, and thinking as a learner within a community of learners, and as a *professional* teacher" (Darling-Hammond et al., 1995, p. 95).

Teachers in PDSs are also actively involved in the redesign and improvement of schools. In such schools, as in career lattices, leadership opportunities are available to all teachers (indeed, leading and learning are embedded aspects of a teacher's role) and are based on experience and expertise (i.e., leadership is not formally assigned). Specifically, teachers are extensively involved in the preparation of preservice teachers and new teachers such as mentoring or teaching at colleges of education. Further, teachers in PDSs work on their own professional development by peer coaching, visiting other schools, or presenting at workshops; collaborate to develop a high-quality education for all through designing instruction to meet diverse learners' needs, creating new assessments, or reviewing new instructional methods; and become involved in continuous inquiry by conducting research with peers and university colleagues, presenting at professional conferences (Darling-Hammond et al., 1995; Teitel, 1997).

Finally, *constructivist leadership* in schools focuses on people collaborating to share ideas and concerns, construct meaning, make sense of their work, and grow together. Action research teams, special working places such as a professional library, and special events like group conversations are structures associated with this approach. Based on constructivist learning theory, such as notions from the works of Dewey, Piaget, Vygotsky, Schon, and Gardner—which posits that learners construct knowledge through social interaction, reflect on these learning experiences, and thus make meaning of their learning—constructivist leadership allows teachers' roles to change and different leaders to emerge according to interest, expertise, the overriding purpose of schooling, and the needs of children, adults, and the community (Lambert et al., 1995).

Emergent teacher leadership has been defined as "Teachers who are leaders lead within and beyond the classroom, influence others toward improved educational practice, and identify with and contribute to a community of leaders" (Katzenmeyer & Moller, 1996, p. 6). To date, only a handful of studies exist that focus on emergent teacher leadership: Corallo, 1995; Darling-Hammond et al., 1995; Heller and Firestone, 1995; Lieberman, 1992; Miller, 1992; Odell, 1997; Phillips, 2004; Stone, Horejs, and Lomas, 1997; Sabatini, 2002; Smylie, 1995; and Teitel, 1997 (Figure 1.4). These studies indicate the following:

- The roles for emergent teacher leaders evolve in natural ways, based on individual school needs.
- These roles are available to all teachers.
- Emergent teacher leaders confront fewer obstacles than teacher leaders holding formal positions, primarily because teachers have more control over relationships with emergent teacher leaders as compared to relationships with administrators or formally appointed teacher leaders.
- The use of select strategies by teacher leaders has the potential to significantly contribute to improvements in teaching and learning.

Figure 1.4   Findings From Research Studies on Emergent Teacher Leadership

Date	Researcher	Focus of Study	Findings
1992	Miller	Development of teacher leadership in a restructured school	• Inquiry, dialogue, reflection, invention, action, and trust became school norms. • Teacher leadership became a school norm. • Classroom teachers, not the formally designated team leaders, initiated most improvement efforts. • Supporting factors included superintendent's and principal's interest, support, and advocacy.
1995	Corallo	Informal teacher leaders who had the ability to influence others	• Factors that influenced the development of informal teacher leaders included family background, success in early leadership experiences, mentor teachers, professional growth activities, and administrative support.
1995	Darling-Hammond et al.	Teacher leadership in Professional Development Schools (PDSs)	• PDSs provided opportunities for all teachers to lead in their areas of expertise and interest (mentors, teacher educators, curriculum developers, decision makers, problem solvers, change agents, researchers). • Teacher leadership was inclusive, not exclusive. • Teacher leadership was not artificial or imposed. • Teacher leadership roles were available to all teachers. • Teacher leadership emerged as a normal role for teachers.
1995	Heller & Firestone	Schools that had successfully institutionalized a problem-solving program	• Principals were not the key leaders for change. • Teachers performed critical leadership functions, including encouraging, reinforcing, monitoring, and educating each other.
1997	Stone et al.	Similarities and differences in teacher leadership at elementary, middle, and high school levels	• In middle schools, teacher leadership was informal, emergent, and voluntary. • Middle school teacher leaders considered themselves catalysts and facilitators. • Teacher leadership improved collaboration, school improvement, and personal and professional growth. • Teacher leadership in a shared decision-making setting formed the basis of collective leadership. • Elementary and high school teacher leaders were formally designated by administrators.
2002	Sabatini	Teachers' perspectives of emergent teacher leadership in an elementary school	• Teachers who were empowered to lead felt trusted, valued, and validated. • Emergent teacher leaders and other teachers interacted in meaningful ways, including sharing, coaching, problem solving, and inquiry (i.e., the focus was on instructional improvement and school improvement). • Teachers identified improved instruction, increased leadership capacity, increased stability, and improved morale as outcomes of experiences with emergent teacher leaders.

Figure 1.4 (Continued)

Date	Researcher	Focus of Study	Findings
2004	Phillips	Emergent teacher leaders' and principals' perspectives of instructional leadership in a successful shared governance elementary school	• Outcomes of collaborative instructional leadership included development of norms of collaboration and collegiality, emergence of teacher leaders, greater accomplishment toward the common purpose, delivery of more effective instructional leadership, strengthening of trust and respect, creation of a positive learning environment, an increase in the sense of ownership and responsibility for outcomes of instructional leaders, and positive impact on instruction.

Before 2002, the work of emergent teacher leaders had not been scientifically linked to classroom or school-level benefits (Smylie & Denny, 1990; Trachtman, 1991; Wasley, 1991). In that year Sabatini (2002) found that interactions between emergent teacher leaders and teachers resulted in improved instruction. However, Sabatini's research was limited to one elementary school that recognized teacher leaders, albeit unofficially, and formally encouraged collaborative inquiry, problem solving, and shared decision making. In another study Phillips (2004) demonstrated that collaborative instructional leadership initiated by emerging teacher leaders and principals yielded norms of collaboration and collegiality, the emergence of teacher leaders, greater progress toward a common purpose, delivery of more effective instructional leadership, strengthening of trust and respect, creation of a positive learning environment, and positive impacts on instruction. Despite promising work, literature that focuses on the nature of emergent teacher leadership is largely exploratory.

THE THIRD SOURCE OF TEACHER HELP: NATURALLY OCCURRING INFORMAL PEER CONSULTATION

There is relatively little empirical evidence concerning the particular characteristics and qualities of relations among teachers . . . that are most conducive to teacher learning and change.

—Smylie & Hart, 1999, p. 425

There is little doubt that formal and quasi-formal approaches to teacher leadership (as discussed earlier) encourage collaborative work and may have some positive effects on teachers and their instruction; this notwithstanding, such approaches can be problematic and costly. Thus *naturally occurring peer consultation,* the third source of teacher help, is potentially efficacious; but it is the least researched source of help for teachers. *This source of teacher support includes informal and emergent interactions and relationships among teachers that significantly facilitate and influence teachers' classroom instruction across school levels and across different governance structures. The teacher is neither designated a* teacher leader, *nor is the teacher given a formal leadership role of any kind.*

We investigated naturally occurring peer consultation among teachers to determine if this form of consultation, reinforced by the social relationships among teachers, actually created and sustained teachers' professional learning and development. (In fact, one major implication of our findings is that teacher learning should address both *what* is learned and *how* it is learned [Carter, 1990; Rosenholtz, 1985], particularly with regard to peer consultation, which we will discuss later.) Chapters 2 through 6 describe in detail the intriguing results of our study of *naturally occurring peer consultation.*

Our Study of Peer Consultation Among Teachers

The study that forms the basis of this book focused on teachers' perspectives on naturally occurring teacher-to-teacher consultation. We examined the actions of peer consultants that teachers indicated directly or indirectly influenced their teaching positively, and specifically, the effects of such actions on teachers' reflection, instruction, and feelings. (Please see Resource: Research Method and Procedures at the end of this book for protocol details.)

We designed the Inventory of Teacher Actions that Positively Influence Your Teaching (ITAPIYT), an open-ended questionnaire, to collect personal meanings about the study topic. The ITAPIYT was administered to 297 elementary, middle, and high school teachers in the southeastern United States. The following instruction appeared on each page of the questionnaire: "Describe in detail *one action* on each of the following pages (what another teacher did) that directly or indirectly helped you teach more effectively. Please give examples to clarify what you mean." In addition, we asked teachers to describe the exact effects of the teacher's action identified above on their thinking, teaching, and feelings. The survey included five pages with the same question; thus a teacher had the opportunity to describe, in detail, up to five actions.

We coded data from the study respondents according to principles for inductive research and comparative analysis (Bogdan & Biklen, 1982; Glaser, 1978, 1998; Glaser & Strauss, 1967; Taylor & Bogdan, 1998). This form of analysis required a comparison of each new unit of data to those coded previously for emergent categories and subcategories. Display matrixes were used to identify and refine conceptual and theoretical ideas derived from the data. This protocol also permitted comparisons of the descriptive and theoretical ideas produced by the study with the relevant extant literature (Bogdan & Biklen, 1982; Fontana & Frey, 2000; Glaser, 1978, 1998; Glaser & Strauss, 1967; Taylor & Bogdan, 1998).

All descriptive, conceptual, and theoretical ideas produced from our study are based on the teachers' perspectives. Because of space limitations, quotes drawn directly from our study data have been used to illustrate select ideas.

The Importance of This Study

This study of peer consultation behaviors that influence teachers' reflection, teaching, and feelings has generated new descriptive, conceptual, and theoretical knowledge in an important area of public education. It also expands the well-established school reform literature by, for example, discussing the effects of informal, emergent, naturally occurring forms of teacher-to-teacher consultation on teachers and their work with students. (Recent studies such as that by Leithwood & Jantzi [2000] have found that formalizing teacher leadership in schools attempting reform along collegial–democratic lines has, at times, actually undermined such efforts.) In addition, such knowledge contributes directly to teacher development by providing detailed descriptions of the nature and effects of peer consultation on teachers. Suggesting pathways to overcome the problem of time for formal teacher collaboration (an example of a critical obstacle to shared leadership and decision making not discussed in the teacher development literature), is one such contribution. Finally, this study is timely in educational leadership given recent research on schools as *caring* and *just* communities in which educators develop mutual trust and respect while working collaboratively toward common goals (Enomoto, 1997) and transformational forms of leadership that promote teacher empowerment for school improvement (Blase & Blase, 2001).

Practically speaking, knowledge about peer consultation and its positive effects on teachers and their work in the classroom can be applied in staff development and university-based programs to sensitize practicing and prospective teachers and administrators to the need to cultivate the development of groups that support peer consultation (Lambert et al., 1995); enhance professional school communities by granting autonomy and providing staff development, time, place, activities, and recognition, for instance (Blase & Blase, 1999); and open communication and positive environment in schools (Katzenmeyer & Moller, 1996).

The results of our study, as presented in this book, will also be a valuable resource for central office personnel and boards of education throughout the United States. Individuals in these positions are legally, professionally, and ethically responsible for school improvement, including student achievement. Unfortunately, the No Child Left Behind Act (NCLB) of 2001 and state mandates have decreased control at the level of the individual school; frequently, the result has been distrust and poor morale among teachers, a state of affairs that must be overcome by capitalizing on teachers' expertise and providing opportunities for collaborative learning. Specifically, our study has implications for the preparation, professional development, and support of teachers and school-level administrators and for developing viable district policies, such as including teachers in decision-making processes, which affects the degree of teacher autonomy and teacher involvement in decisions important to their work, and providing flexible development opportunities. The role of central office personnel and boards of education are especially important in light of related reform efforts that mandate standards, high-stakes testing, and consequences for schools that *fail* because such factors effectively limit teachers' roles in school improvement.

A Portrait of Peer Consultation

> *The purpose of consultation is to stimulate self-evaluation and critical thinking.*
>
> —Holt, 1992, p. 3

In general we found that from the teachers' perspectives, peer consultation builds school-based teacher cultures characterized by robust forms of teacher collaboration and collegiality and results in teacher development, teacher confidence, and school effectiveness and improvement, the advantages of which have been described by several researchers (Lieberman & Miller, 1999; Mortimore, Sammons, Stoll, Lewis, & Ecob, 1988). Hargreaves (1994), for example, reported that effective collaborative school cultures among teachers tended to be spontaneous, voluntary, development oriented, pervasive across time and space, and unpredictable; such cultures included principals who created a sense of school unity, modeled expectations for teachers, valued teachers, adjusted schedules to facilitate shared planning time, and encouraged experimentation. This, in turn, helped teachers break down barriers, work closely together, and learn from each other while participating on externally and internally initiated projects. Hargreaves, however, has noted that attempts to create *formal* collaborative cultures, in reality, frequently produced cultures of congeniality, complacency, and comfort. Said differently, truly *collaborative cultures* can be contrasted with other forms of teacher culture, including fragmented individualism, balkanization, contrived collegiality, and a moving mosaic (Figure 1.5). Perhaps the best example of effective collaboration among teachers is that of *lesson study* among Japanese teachers, wherein teachers collectively observe and study each other's lessons to develop instructional expertise and build the capacity for collegial learning; yet such collaboration occurs in a culture imbued with the notion of improvement through collective effort and critical self-reflection (Lewis, Perry, & Murata, 2003).

Figure 1.5   Forms of Teacher Culture

1. *Fragmented individualism*

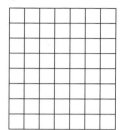

- Isolation
- Ceiling to improvement
- Protection from outside interference

2. *Balkanization*

- City states
- Inconsistencies
- Loyalties and identities tied to particular group
- Whole is less than sum of its parts

3. *Collaborative culture*

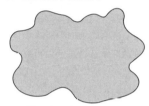

- Sharing, trust, support
- Central to daily work
- "Family" structure may involve paternalistic or maternalistic leadership
- Joint work
- Continuous improvement

4. *Contrived collegiality*

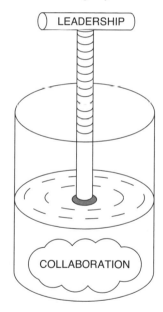

- Strategy for creating collegiality
- Also strategy for contriving and controlling it
- Administrative procedure
- Safe simulation
- A device that can suppress desire

5. *The moving mosaic*

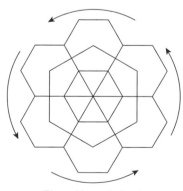

- Blurred boundaries
- Overlapping categories and membership
- Flexible, dynamic, responsive
- Also uncertain, vulnerable, contested

SOURCE: A. Hargreaves (1994). *Changing teachers, changing times: Teachers' work and culture in the postmodern age,* p. 238. New York: Teachers College Press. Used with permission.

Is a Peer Consultant a Supervisor, a Mentor, or a Coach?

We found that the natural, spontaneous, facilitative, collaborative encounters between peer consultants and teachers defied description as supervision, mentoring, or coaching. Therefore we refer to teachers' work with colleagues as peer consultation. What are the differences? First, *supervisors* are judges with the power to direct teachers' behaviors, whereas peer consultants respect teachers' autonomy. (This is certainly not to say that, on occasion, weak teachers must be directly supervised by administrators.) Second, *mentors* act on established standards and often work under constraints of limited preparation and time, whereas peer consultants are not bound by predetermined standards that may be irrelevant to a particular teacher's classroom context and student needs; further, peer consultants share their expertise, availing themselves of whatever opportunities for consulting that arise. Third, *coaches* have special preparation for work with colleagues and transfer prescribed approaches or processes to teachers. In contrast, we found that peer consultants—who may not have expertise specific to a given teacher's work or a specific focus for dialogue other than that selected by the teacher—naturally observed and conferred with teachers in a consultative, facilitative, and nonthreatening manner. In essence, the focus for the peer consultant is idiosyncratic to the teaching context and the teacher's concerns; the peer consultant helped the teacher identify a relevant focus, assess progress, and improve teaching in a timely manner. Peer consultants were not *neutral observers* who withheld their judgments and suggestions; they were *full partners* in a peer dialogue and often revealed their opinions and encouraged teachers to confront differing perceptions and perspectives through constructive-reflective dialogue (Goldsberry, 1998).

Discussing teachers' craft knowledge, Grimmett and MacKinnon (1992) point out that such knowledge "represents teachers' judgment in apprehending the events of practice from their own perspectives as students of teaching and learning, much as a 'glue' that brings all of the knowledge bases to bear on the act of teaching" (p. 387), and this knowledge is a "construction of situated, learner-focused, procedural and content-related pedagogical knowledge" (p. 393). Thus, peer consultants could be considered *knowers* of the craft of teaching.

We also found that peer consultants often engaged in reciprocal observation. Garmston (1987) aptly described this as collegial coaching, which is contextualized and focused on self-reflection and professional dialogue and, as Hargreaves & Dawe (1990) have stated, "the focus for improvement is not determined externally" (p. 231). See Figure 1.6 for Goldsberry's (1998) description of the types of helping roles discussed previously, which are listed according to the degree of teacher involvement.

Figure 1.6   Helping Roles

Supervisor

- Sets boundaries for teacher autonomy
- Has authority to *remediate* if teacher crosses spoken (or even unspoken) boundaries
- Has organizational blessing to direct teaching behavior using own experience and preferences as a guide

Mentor

- Advises teacher of established (by policy or norm) boundaries
- Advises according to established standards if teacher crosses spoken (or unspoken) boundaries
- Informs supervisor if actions outside of boundaries continue

Coach

- Advises teacher of boundaries inherent in skill or approach being coached
- Uses coach's understandings of the proper application of the method as the standards
- Determines *rightness* of teaching method
- Reports teacher's proficiency if necessary with method to supervisor or to mentor

Consultant

- Serves at request of teacher
- Advises teacher regarding *goodness* of practice
- Accords teacher the liberty to act upon or to ignore advice
- Accords teacher the liberty to determine standards
- Challenges teacher's reasoning when appropriate, but (barring malpractice) allows teacher's reasoning to prevail

---

SOURCE: Adapted from "Teacher involvement in supervision" (p. 432), by L. F. Goldsberry, 1998, in *Handbook of Research on School Supervision*, G. R. Firth & E. F. Pajak (Eds.) (pp. 428–462). New York: Simon & Schuster Macmillan.

What Happens During Peer Consultation?

Good teaching looks effortless because a teacher's knowledge and experience are invisible! We all know, however, that teaching is a tricky blend of knowledge and action, a way of contextualizing knowledge. Good teaching is, in fact, complex and challenging, and even the best teachers face difficulties translating formal knowledge into effective practice. To use Schön's (1987) metaphor, teachers face the challenge of fusing the hard ground of scientific methodology with the swamp of messy problems of practice.

We found that peer consultants became the *other*, helping a teacher use research and practice reflectively (Fenstermacher & Richardson (1993); the peer consultant frequently became the critical friend (Kroath, 1990), whose dialogue with the teacher

- supported and confirmed the reality of classroom experience,
- challenged assumptions about practice,
- encouraged the teacher to elaborate on her/his practical reasoning that undergirds action,
- tapped teachers' knowledge, and
- ensured that practice is contextualized and justified.

Peer consultation was effective because both consultants and teachers brought their experiential knowledge as well as their ability to acquire new knowledge to bear on the classroom teaching being examined. In effect, they used their collective knowledge to gain new knowledge. Munby, Russell, and Martin (2001) described teachers' experiential knowledge as a rich amalgam of constructs including situated knowledge, event-structured knowledge, personal practical knowledge, images, and knowing-in-action. Teachers acquire experiential knowledge constructs through tacit understandings, reflection, authority of experience, nested knowing, reframing, and developed expertise; this is demonstrated in the differences among preservice, neophyte, and experienced teachers. This is further enhanced by the metaphors, voice, and, in particular, the craft knowledge teachers bring to the dialogue. See Figure 1.7 for a description of teachers' rationales for peer consultation, which suggests that practical reasoning—coupled with experiential knowledge and adapted to context by dialogue among teachers—results in shared learning for innovation and improvement.

What Are the Metagoals of Peer Consultation?

Our study of teachers demonstrates that peer consultation is critical to school innovation and improvement because

- teaching is dynamic, situated, complex, contextualized work;
- teachers flourish in a culture of shared learning;
- teachers learn from each other's expertise and knowledge; and
- teachers spontaneously consult with each other to solve the immediate problems of teaching and learning.

Further, we found that the critical process factors in peer consultation included

- developing a positive, collegial relationship among peers,
- using frequent (if possible) and usually casual contact,
- using contemporaneous data from classroom teaching and learning,
- implementing teacher reflection, and
- using teacher control of decisions and implementation.

Figure 1.7   Teachers' Rationales for Peer Consultation

Because teaching . . .

- Is dynamic, situated, complex, contextualized work
- Is about working with diverse learners
- Unfolds in practice
- Requires continuous decision making and problem solving

We must . . .

- Develop trust
- Create opportunities to discuss experiences and knowledge
- Foster dialogic discourse
- Develop a culture of shared learning rather than a culture of isolation
- Engage in continuous learning from each other
- Engage in critical collaborative processes
- Engage in social sharing
- Nurture sharing
- Develop a recursive, problem-based, collaboration of practitioners
- Become an interdependent learning community of informal, self-constituting, naturally occurring, spontaneous relationships among practitioners
- Help each other fill the unfilled gaps in knowledge
- Not be discounted, diminished, inhibited, or marginalized by others

So we can . . .

- Access teachers' expertise
- Access unarticulated knowledge learned in work
- Move from tacit knowledge to explicit knowledge
- Generate improvisational knowledge
- Adapt knowledge
- Mobilize knowledge
- Amplify knowledge throughout our school
- Solve problems of teaching and learning
- Ask new questions
- Search for new perspectives
- Craft new explanations
- Cobble together innovative solutions
- Spontaneously solve problems
- Do what works

Thus, spontaneous collaborations among teachers . . .

- Contain innovative knowledge
- Are critical to school innovation and improvement
- Influence the way work progresses

SOURCE: Blase & Blase, 2004b. For further study see Brown & Duguid, 1991; Bryk & Schneider, 2002; Daft & Weick, 1984; Fullan, 2003; Lave & Wenger, 1991; Nonaka, 1994; Shellard, 2003.

Given the importance of spontaneous processes embedded in peer consultation, we recommend the following as the natural metagoals of peer consultation:

- heighten job performance,
- refine skills,
- provide opportunities for meaningful discussion about teaching practices, and
- provide mutual benefit.

In the broadest sense, we found that peer consultation enhanced teachers' self-efficacy (teachers' belief in their own abilities and capacity to successfully solve teaching and learning problems) as they reflected on practice and grew together, and it also encouraged a bias for action (improvement through collaboration) on the part of teachers.

What Do Peer Consultants Do? The Five Skills of Our Peer Consultation Model

From our analyses of naturally occurring peer consultation, we developed the PCM; this model depicts the five major elements of peer consultants' work with teachers described in subsequent chapters of this book. Generally speaking, this type of collaborative work resulted in substantial learning and improvement for both teachers and peer consultants, a phenomenon also described by Joyce & Showers (2002). We learned that the collective work of peer colleagues frequently included effective communication, caring, and developing trust (Chapter 2) and knowledge of and ability to use teaching strategies that, according to the professional literature, promote student achievement (Chapters 3 and 4). Additional skills derived from our study data—showing and sharing (Chapter 5) and guiding for classroom management (Chapter 6)—complete our model. In Chapter 7 we discuss ways educators can capitalize on the power of peer consultation.

Peer Consultation Model: Five Skills

1. Building healthy relationships by communicating, caring, and developing trust
2. Exploiting the knowledge base
3. Planning and organizing for learning
4. Showing and sharing
5. Guiding for classroom management

A Call to Action

A decade ago Lieberman (1995) lamented the limitations of traditional approaches to teacher development and argued the following:

- Teachers' professional development has been limited by lack of knowledge about how teachers learn.
- Teaching has been described as a set of technical skills, leaving little room for invention and the building of craft knowledge.
- Professional development opportunities have often ignored the critical importance of the context within which teachers work.
- Teachers' definitions of the problems of practice have often been ignored.
- Strategies for change have often not considered the importance of support mechanisms and the necessity of learning over time.
- Time and the necessary mechanisms for inventing, as well as consuming, new knowledge have often been absent from schools.
- The move from *direct teaching* to facilitating *in-school learning* has not been linked to longer-term strategies aimed at both changing teaching practice and changing school culture.
- There has been a lack of networks, collaboratives, and partnerships that provide teachers with professional learning communities that support changes in teaching practices.
- The agenda for reform involves teachers in practices that have not been part of the accepted view of teachers' professional learning. (Lieberman, 1995, pp. 595–596)

Lieberman (1995) further noted that successful educational reform requires that teachers have "opportunities to discuss, think about, try out, and hone new practices"; she called for continuous learning among teachers in the context of the school and classroom, and she suggested that teachers can learn about teaching and learning by

- building new roles—teacher leader, peer coach, or teacher researcher, for example;
- creating new structures such as problem-solving groups or decision-making teams;
- working on new tasks including journal and proposal writing, learning about assessment, creating standards, and analyzing or writing case studies of practice; and
- creating a culture of inquiry, wherein professional learning is expected, sought after, and an ongoing part of teaching and school life. (Lieberman, 1995, p. 593)

In the past 10 years, Lieberman's concerns and suggestions have not been widely heeded; nevertheless, a shift in the dialogic plates of teacher development and reflection on teaching appears to be under way. The third source of teacher help, peer consultation, shows potential for great school improvement. Indeed, the study described in this book makes clear that teachers find peer consultation among colleagues to be the crux, indeed, the very heart of school improvement. In peer consultation, teachers spontaneously, gently, and skillfully help each other; teachers teach teachers about teaching and teachers collaboratively solve the complex problems of teaching in today's schools. This is a natural marriage of self-help and spirit among teachers whose time has come. This book is an exploration into that world, the world of peer consultation.

SUMMARY

This chapter first presented our concept of peer consultation drawn directly from our study data. Discussions of three primary sources of teacher assistance—principals, lead teachers, and peer consultants—was followed by a very brief outline of the research method and procedures used to conduct our study of peer consultation. Some of our most important findings were highlighted in the first pages of this chapter. Peer consultation skill #1, building healthy relationships by communicating, caring, and developing trust, is the focus of Chapter 2.

QUESTIONS TO CONSIDER

1. Are teachers in your school at different developmental stages, ages, and points in their careers? How do these differences impact their professional development needs? What can be done to create relevant professional development opportunities for all of your teachers?

2. In what ways do professional staff development programs in your school adhere to the principles of adult development and to the National Staff Development Council's 12 Standards? What can you do to ensure that such programs reflect these principles and standards?

3. Which of the three sources of teacher assistance discussed in this chapter are used in your school? What can you do to extend peer consultation as a form of teacher assistance?

4. Do teachers in your school have meaningful discussions about lessons and problems of teaching? If not, what can you do to create such opportunities?

SUGGESTED READING FOR FURTHER LEARNING

Group Development

Martinez, M. C. (2004) *Teachers working together for school success.* Thousand Oaks, CA: Corwin Press. [This discusses how teachers can influence each other, handle conflict, and work together to build a stronger school community.]

Wheelan, S. (2004). *Faculty groups: From frustration to collaboration.* Thousand Oaks, CA: Corwin Press. [This discusses how to help faculty groups become productive.]

Professional Learning Communities

DuFour, R. (2003). *Building a professional learning community.* Arlington, VA: American Association of School Administrators. [This discusses roles and strategies for principals, teachers, parents, and professional developers.]

Martin-Kniep, G. (2004). *Developing learning communities through teacher expertise.* Thousand Oaks, CA: Corwin Press. [This outlines how to build a reflective, collaborative environment and develop standards-based curriculum and assessment.]

Roberts, S. M., & Pruitt, E. Z. (2003). *Schools as professional learning communities: Collaborative activities and strategies for professional development.* Thousand Oaks, CA: Corwin Press. [This is a primer on how to work with teachers, parents, and administrators to build a learning community.]

Beginning Teacher Assistance

Gordon, P., & Maxey, S. (2000). *How to help beginning teachers succeed.* Alexandria, VA: Association for Supervision and Curriculum

Development. [This presents a design of a beginning teacher assistance program]

Mentoring

Daresh, J. C. (2003). *Teachers mentoring teachers: A practical approach to helping new and experienced staff.* Thousand Oaks, CA: Corwin Press. [This deals with how to plan, implement, and evaluate mentor programs.]

Jonson, K. F. (2002). *Being an effective mentor: How to help beginning teachers succeed.* Thousand Oaks, CA: Corwin Press. [This is comprehensive and practical handbook for teachers and administrators.]

Instructional Leadership and Teacher Empowerment

Blase, J., & Blase, J. (2001). *Empowering teachers: What successful principals do* (2nd ed.). Thousand Oaks, CA: Corwin Press. [This discusses how to promote teacher empowerment and to enhance teaching and learning.]

Blase, J. & Blase, J. (2004). *Handbook of instructional leadership: How successful principals promote teaching and learning* (2nd ed.). Thousand Oaks, CA: Corwin Press. [This details how to effectively promote teaching and school improvement.]

Teachers' Work

Hargreaves, A. (1994). *Changing teachers, changing times: Teachers' work and culture in the postmodern age.* New York: Teachers College Press. [This identifies the complexity and dilemmas of teaching and posits the need to change the structures and cultures of teaching.]

Lieberman, A., & Miller, J. (1999). *Teachers—Transforming their world and their work.* New York: Teachers College. [This addresses the realities of schools and teaching and focuses on constraints and possibilities in teachers' work.]

Teacher Leadership

Crowther, F., Kaagan, S. S., Ferguson, M., & Hann, L. (2002). *Developing teacher leaders: How teacher leadership enhances school success.* Thousand Oaks, CA: Corwin Press. [This discusses how to redefine and elevate teachers' roles.]

Katzenmeyer, M., & Moller, G. (2001). *Awakening the sleeping giant: Helping teachers develop as leaders* (2nd ed.) Thousand Oaks, CA: Corwin Press. [This discusses how to develop teacher leaders who lead within and beyond the classroom.]

Peer Coaching

Allen, D. W., & LeBlanc, A. C. (2004). *Collaborative peer coaching that improves instruction: The 2+2 performance appraisal model.* Thousand Oaks, CA: Corwin Press. [This presents a method in which teachers visit each other's classrooms and provide two compliments and two suggestions for improvement to each other.]

2

Peer Consultation Skill #1: Building Healthy Relationships by Communicating, Caring, and Developing Trust

Skillful pairs build trust by acknowledging and deferring to one another's knowledge and skill and by talking to each other in ways that preserve natural dignity, and by giving their work together a full measure of energy, thought, and attention.

—Little, 1985, p. 35

Trust . . . is established more by deeds than by words. [It] is built between two people when each person is convinced that the other is both motivated and competent to sustain the relationship.

—Schmuck & Runkel, 1994, p. 127

The focus of this chapter is on peer consultation skill #1, building healthy relationships by communicating, caring, and developing trust. We begin with a discussion of the four key types of peer collaboration described in the professional literature. We then present our findings about the importance of establishing effective communication, taking a caring approach to peer interaction, and building trust by engaging in nonthreatening, open conversations as teachers engage in peer consultation. The chapter ends with a brief description of development activities for teachers and administrators.

COMMUNICATION AS THE KEY

Current research in education reveals significant findings about teacher development and school improvement:

- Effective teaching behavior is correlated with student learning (Rowan, Chiang, & Miller, 1997).
- Teachers are instrumental to successful school-based change efforts.
- When teachers' professional development activities occur in isolation from each other or from teachers' regular classroom experiences, such activities rarely have any impact on teaching and student learning (Guskey & Sparks, 1996).
- When teachers have opportunities to share their thinking about teaching and learning and opportunities to search for solutions to teaching and learning problems, they are more likely to engage in productive, collegial endeavors and experimentation (Little, 1981).

Further, as Stigler and Heibert (1999) have noted, "Not only are they [teachers] the gatekeepers for all improvement efforts, they are also in the best position to acquire the knowledge that is needed. They are, after all, the only ones who can improve teaching" (p. 174). *In essence, then, student learning and school development are predicated on teachers' collaboration— teacher talk.*

Typically, however, teachers' opportunities for talking, collaborating, reviewing their work, discussing student learning derived from their work, and posing questions for additional inquiry are severely limited (DuFour & Eaker, 1998). Coaching programs, for example, have failed to achieve their potential because they lack time to develop mutually respectful relationships (Wade, 1985), pressure from superiors to obtain information that could be used against coachees, the tendency for coaches to offer quick fixes that ignore the complexity of teaching and learning, and fears and rivalries among teachers. It seems that efforts to develop teacher collaboration often fall short in staff development and formal coaching programs in which collaboration is a specific goal! In this chapter we explore the range of definitions of peer consultation found in the professional literature as well as our findings about peer consultation skill #1, communication, caring, and developing trust; and we describe related effects on teachers.

FOUR TYPES OF PEER CONSULTATION

As we analyzed results of our study, we began to wonder, How are teachers who are peer consultants able to discuss student learning, develop their own collaborative norms and strategies, and hold themselves accountable for their own work—all on the fly? Interestingly, the results of our study indicate that *communication* was the key; further, the communication among teachers involved in peer consultation was neither limited by nor embedded in staff development or formal coaching programs. Rather, it was a natural outgrowth among professionals who assumed that they could help others improve. Peer consultation was a natural blend of the technical and human aspects of teaching; the amount of time spent was much less important than the quality of the interaction. In the following text, we discuss several types of peer consultation identified in the extant literature in terms of our findings; you will note that all rely on effective interpersonal communication.

Acheson, Shamsher, and Smith (1998) identified four types of peer consultation:

Type #1: *peer coaching* that focuses on the principles of teaching or teacher effectiveness;

Type #2: *peer coaching* that focuses on the models of teaching;

Type #3: *peer consultation* that focuses on instructional fine tuning, reflective practice, and innovation; and

Type #4: *peer consultation* that focuses on organizational development and change processes.

In the following text, we briefly describe each type of coaching and consultation.

Type #1: Peer Coaching With a Focus on
Principles of Teaching or Teacher Effectiveness

Peer teachers from inside or outside the school help teachers learn to use specific teaching behaviors, which comprise a comprehensive system of instruction based on Madeline Hunter's synthesis of the teacher effectiveness literature. They may also use, for example, Cummings' Teacher Effectiveness Training, derived from research on student learning. Teachers assist each other but do not focus on developing teachers' self-assessment or critical reflection skills.

Type #2: Peer Coaching With Focus on Models of Teaching

Peer teachers critique each other with a focus on fidelity to a specific teaching model (chosen among many models). The observing teacher didactically teaches, rather than consulting with peers.

Type #3: Peer Consultation With Focus on Fine Tuning, Reflective Practice, and Innovation

Designed to promote teachers' opportunities for general reflection, refinement of teaching, and critical self-analysis, this highly collegial and reciprocal approach is not focused on learning a specific system of teaching skills but on an eclectic approach to teaching.

Type #4: Peer Consultation With Focus on Organizational Development and Change

With the goal of promoting a healthy school climate for change, teachers develop communication, problem-solving, and decision-making skills, among others, to ensure the success of instructional innovations.

The peer consultation reported by teachers in our study subsumed all four of the aforementioned types: Elements of the first two appeared in consultants' and teachers' efforts to use scientific or technical approaches to collegial work, and elements of the latter two appeared in consultants' and teachers' development of supportive relationships and reflection on teaching. We found that the most frequently used helping behaviors of peer consultants are similar to those identified with the third type of peer consultation; these are also consistent with behaviors associated with the British Columbia Teachers' Federation's Program for Quality Teaching (PQT) and include the following:

- Blending systematic analysis of teaching and intuitive professional knowledge;
- Avoiding judgment of colleagues' work (because it diminishes self-evaluation as well as the confidence and trust needed for risk taking and experimentation with new solutions to teaching and learning problems);
- Developing supportive communication, mutual respect, and reciprocity to foster a safe climate in which to collaborate;
- Believing that teachers have the power to understand, challenge, and transform their teaching practices;
- Maintaining the perspective of "observing as if you were B. F. Skinner and giving feedback as if you were Carl Rogers" (Acheson et al., 1998, p. 773); and
- Assuming that strict control by administrators is unnecessary for improved teacher awareness and critical reflection.

According to Acheson and colleagues, type #3 peer consultation, with its solid foundation of good communication, results in high levels of satisfaction and closer relationships among colleagues through collaboration.

On the whole, we found that effective communication and its resulting caring between peer consultants and teachers significantly increased interpersonal trust, a remarkable experience that further enhanced teachers' sense of community as well as their teaching and students' learning. In effect, by engaging in effective forms of communication, peer consultants and teachers reduced the isolation common to their professional experience. In this chapter we explore several peer consultant skills revealed in our data, including communicating, caring, and developing trust.

PEER CONSULTANTS' COMMUNICATION STYLES

In general, we discovered that peer consultants and teachers practiced the seven types of effective communication described by Schmuck and Runkel (1994), including active listening, paraphrasing (checking for meaning), impression checking (checking for understanding of feelings), describing another's behavior, describing personal behavior, clearly stating personal ideas, and describing personal feelings. In so doing, peer consultants engaged in *freeing responses* with each other and avoided *binding responses* (Figure 2.1).

Figure 2.1   Freeing Versus Binding Responses in Interpersonal Communication

FREEING RESPONSES

- Listening attentively rather than merely remaining silent
- Paraphrasing and checking your impressions of the other's inner state
- Seeking information to understand the other
- Offering information that is relevant to the other's concern
- Describing observable behaviors that influence you
- Directly reporting your feelings
- Offering your opinions or stating your value position

BINDING RESPONSES

- Changing the subject without explanation
- Interpreting the other's behavior by describing unchangeable experiences or qualities
- Advising or persuading
- Vigorously agreeing or obligating the other with "how could you?"

From the teachers' perspective, use of these seven types of communication resulted in casual, comfortable exchanges between peer consultants and teachers characterized by mutual reflective dialogue about teaching and learning; focusing on student learning; openness to improvement; listening; storytelling; sharing individual points of view; voicing individual concerns; discussing communication and relationship norms; solving problems; making suggestions and decisions; questioning practice; discovering opportunities; encouraging each other; demonstrating caring, empathy, and genuineness; empowering one another; raising professional and personal expectations, and finding deeper meaning in individual work.

PEER CONSULTANTS' CARING

To care for another person, in the most significant sense, is to help him grow and actualize himself.

—Mayeroff, 1971, p. 1

Caring teachers are attentive and receptive to students, helpful in solving students' problems, and dedicated to promoting students' growth (Noddings, 1992); we also found that peer consultants demonstrated caring in their work with colleague teachers. Peer consultants respected and encouraged teachers, and this approach substantially elevated pedagogy and increased implementation of school rules and policies. Caring peer consultants were colearners; they attempted to be understanding listeners, creative problem solvers, and mediators and advocates. (Caring in schools, of course, is not only essential to relationships between teachers; it is also central to effective relationships between teachers and school administrators [Blase & Blase, 2004a]. "Leadership is never about ruling others; leadership is about serving others" [Pellicer, 1999, p. 71]; and good school leaders provide teachers with support, trust, and caring.)

Do caring interactions with peer consultants affect teachers' satisfaction and student learning? Do teachers actually learn from colleagues? The answer to both questions is yes. In schools where teachers and principals share a commitment to examining and improving teaching, students tend to be more engaged and more able to do challenging work (Floden, 2001). Participants in our study (who in some cases did not have principal support for their naturally occurring facilitation with colleagues) reported that peer consultants' caring and support positively affected their satisfaction, sense of security, and comfort as well as their teaching and student learning. Such effects are similar to those associated with *guided dialogue* (Pugach, 1990), verbal guidance, metacognitive modeling, and reflective thinking by preservice teachers; this was especially true when teachers faced instructional problems for which they had not developed appropriate forms of self-directed, inner speech associated with reflective teaching (Tharp & Gallimore, 1988).

Beck (1994) has asserted that to contribute to the welfare of the school community, all stakeholders must acknowledge the interrelatedness of people; the importance of developing a sense of community; the importance of promoting human development; and the importance of participating in caring relationships, which she defined as relationships in which people see the potential in others and support and nurture that potential. Accordingly, caring for the teachers in our study consisted of peer consultants' concern for both students and teachers, modeling of high expectations, and assistance in developing a philosophy of teaching.

Concern for Students and Teachers

The teachers we studied were impressed by the consistency of their peer consultants' sensitive regard for children, and this became a model for them:

I watched her praise every student in some way every day; I marveled at how she did it and have tried to follow her example. It may be a smile when they enter the room, a thumbs-up when they remember to push their chairs in, or a positive comment during the class like great work. It may be a comment to the student's homeroom teacher like, "Sam really worked hard today," or "Susan was a big help today."

The teacher's personal involvement with each individual student encouraged me to develop personal relationships with my students. This teacher treated every child as if he or she were her own; she loved them and took an interest in their home life as well as their learning styles.

I learned much from observing his general demeanor. He was very patient and cognizant of student feelings. He had empathy for students, even if their feelings were misguided or unjustified.

One of the most profound experiences of my career involved a fellow educator sharing a movie with us. It was about a child who had apparently died because no one knew him or cared about him.

Peer consultants also expressed heartfelt caring for teachers, even those they did not personally know. To illustrate, one teacher was thrilled by the interest a colleague (who later became her peer consultant) showed in her:

She asked me, "What exactly do you do?" and I explained that speech therapy is about improving communication—not just speech. Then she asked me if she could observe me one day; I was so surprised and I said, "Sure!"

Other teachers discussed caring in terms of the sense of colleagueship they found with peer consultants:

> When we are sitting around in the work room, we always talk to each other about things we have seen or heard or read about and make connections to pieces of literature or parts of the curriculum; it triggers discussion.

> She taught me that we work as a team; we do big things like helping to handle a discipline problem and little things like watching a class so that the teacher can go to the restroom; we always have praise for each other and a pat on the back. We are listeners for each other and we don't judge or gossip.

Peer consultants demonstrated caring in other ways as well, such as providing assurances:

> She was a little older than me and she inspired me after we had had a very rough year and I thought of taking a job elsewhere; she told me not to do it and asked me why I had entered education. I told her I loved it and I wished that other people would value it. She said there is your answer; you don't need to leave.

> I had been worried about saying the wrong thing to a student who was potentially in crisis; my supporting teacher assured me that I was probably the most positive person in that child's life and anything I did would be important. She said that I should reflect later on what I may have said or done differently.

> My teammate often encourages me, especially after a difficult grade level meeting.

Caring was expressed by encouraging teachers through recognition, praise, and positive feedback:

> He published one of my short stories in the school literary magazine; his belief in me as a writer made me believe that I could write, no one had ever made me feel like that before. Now I hope to publish a children's book one day.

> She praised me in front of a group of fellow educators; she specifically identified strategies and personal characteristics that she felt made me an effective teacher and she described me as someone the staff trusted and respected.

> We observe classrooms. The teachers give each other support and compliment each other's teaching.

One day a fellow teacher commented that a certain student always seemed happy and that her parents were requesting that their children be placed in my class for the next year.

Caring was exhibited by providing practical help to teachers:

I was experiencing some serious health problems, but I went to work almost every day. I was sick and didn't realize that I needed surgery until close to spring break. I tried not to let anyone know I was having so much difficulty but one of my colleagues could tell something was wrong. She took it upon herself to help me with various tasks like copying materials, getting grades in on time or covering class for a few minutes now and then to give me a chance to rest.

He donated his carpentry skills and time to help conduct a screening test for my Latin classes.

She took on some responsibilities I had that did not relate to my teaching when I was loaded down with extra tasks; it allowed me to stop worrying so I could teach and I did a much better job for those few days.

She observed my lessons and noted that I had more time on task than she did; she wanted me to help her develop a similar plan for her room. She told me she liked the way that I used my time during small groups.

Teachers also described simple expressions of concern from peer consultants as caring:

My daughter was quite sick and I had spent the day watching as they ran fluids into her body through IVs. I had just come home late in the evening when the phone rang; another teacher was calling to check on me. She didn't know how serious the situation was, but I began to talk about it; mostly I talked about work when she said, I didn't call to talk about work, only to check on you.

Peer consultants demonstrated caring for teachers and students as they discussed and modeled high academic expectations of themselves and for their students. One peer consultant remembered the first time a teacher had done this for her and noted how she worked to do the same for her students:

She told me, "I am an African American and I was always expected to be on the lower track, but I took the highest-level courses available. One elderly English teacher challenged me; she stared at me and said this is an advanced course and if you can't do the work you need to go to the counselor. I knew she was talking to me, but I took it as a personal challenge to prove to her that I would earn an A. Now I tell all of my students that they are smart and they can do what they set their minds to do, and I am proud to share that with my current colleagues."

In addition, some of the teachers we studied reported contrasting examples of low expectations exhibited by other teachers; this emphasized the crucial nature of aiming high academically:

He told me that it really didn't matter what I taught to the low level classes; he claimed they wouldn't learn it anyway.

"Anything is better than what they have," he said. His low expectations made me aware of a profound problem that exists in education today. I want to always give my best effort to all students. I would realize that the brighter, high level students often learned despite who is standing in front of the class, and that the slower students needed not only fine teachers but also challenges.

Speaking of a disruptive student in a classroom, a teacher said, "Let's move quickly to get him into special education so that he no longer disrupts the rest of the students in the class and so they can learn."

An emotionally and behaviorally disabled student was struggling in language arts; I recommended him for help with his reading, but the reading teacher said she could not and would not and did not want to teach him in her program because he couldn't learn and she wouldn't get results; it infuriated me, made me fight to get him into her program. These are the types of children who need these programs the most.

Overall, peer consultants expressed caring by sharing and demonstrating their wisdom—the essence of their philosophy of teaching—gleaned from years of successful experience:

She taught me to "love it or leave it."

She told me to "be yourself."

He constantly said, "We are good enough to admit our mistakes and to correct them."

Among other things, peer consultants' caring for teachers helped to diminish their loneliness and angst in the midst of work problems and issues:

She came by several times a day to check on me and see if my day was going alright; there is nothing worse than loneliness and thinking that no one knows or cares that you're alive.

In the new school, I didn't know anyone; I would have been sentenced to days of isolation if it were not for that teacher and certain others who took the time to stop by.

When I first began teaching, he suggested I not overwhelm myself by taking too much home too often. It has helped me tremendously; I don't feel burned out now, four years later. My work does not trickle into my private life too often; most of my friends who have been teaching are burned out because their work consumes most of their free time.

She told me when it was time to go home.

Last, our study participants painfully described how they witnessed the uncaring treatment of students by teachers, which made them more appreciative of their peer consultants' caring behaviors; these uncaring behaviors reflected disregard, humiliation, and even degradation of students:

A fellow teacher is the model of what I never want to become as a teacher; she is not connected personally in any way with any students nor are the students actively engaged in their learning. The students leave my class with tummy aches and headaches, dreading what is to come in her class.

She showed favoritism toward certain students in her classroom; it was extremely obvious that students considered more popular by her were treated with great respect; less popular students were literally ignored. She wouldn't even look them in the eyes while talking to them.

This teacher criticized a student's project in front of the entire class. Another student blurted out that she shouldn't have done that and the teacher became angry and yelled at him, too.

This teacher never gave the student much of a chance at succeeding. She would point her out as doing the wrong things and made a negative example of her. Often her comments would elicit a laugh from the class; the student was very aware of this.

She called the student up to the front of the classroom, held up her paper and announced to the class that she had received an F.

She rarely smiled, was mostly unpleasant. One day on the playground she accused a student of something that the student hadn't done. Having been taught to always respect people in authority the student stood quietly as she ranted and raved and then slapped her on the cheek. This experience of degradation must still exist in that student's memory.

One of my colleagues was so negative in the way that he approached his students; he complained about their attitudes and their sub-par performance. He didn't let his students have any personality in his classroom, and he was very inflexible. His pessimism carried over to his classroom.

PEER CONSULTANTS BUILDING TRUST

Bryk and Schneider (2002) found that academically high performing schools were more likely to have higher levels of trust among principals, teachers, students, and parents; and trust was linked to improved student outcomes, including test scores. Indeed, a nurturing school has the following characteristics:

> There is trust and caring among all individuals and supportive relationships exist in a positive environment. There is a sense of community where all individuals are valued, participate in decision-making process, and are respected and nurtured, with everyone accepting responsibility for student success. (Green, 1998, p. 9)

Trust is "one party's willingness to be vulnerable to another party based on the confidence that the latter party is (a) benevolent, (b) reliable, (c) competent, (d) honest, and (e) open" (Tschannen-Moran & Hoy, 2000, p. 556). Among teachers, trust is built by collaborating to achieve school and district standards; participating in learning activities, teamwork, and school initiatives; and being collaborative and candid in conversations about teaching and learning (Bryk & Schneider, 2002).

According to our data, a range of peer consultant behaviors helped build trust:

- expressing caring and unconditional support of teachers;
- frankly and directly describing classroom observations;
- openly offering thoughts and opinions; inviting teachers to express opinions, perspectives, and thinking;
- giving teachers time for reflection;
- sharing feelings (e.g., frustrations as well as joys of teaching);
- linking data and information to student learning;

- providing examples and applications;
- discussing ways in which the teacher's work was effective and relevant;
- helping teachers clarify their thinking;
- being nonjudgmental; and
- giving warm feedback that validates teachers (see Martin-Kniep [2004] for details about giving *warm* feedback).

In contrast, many teachers in our study cited negative incidents from past experiences when trust was noticeably absent among teachers; these incidents were painfully etched in their memories and served to heighten their appreciation of trust among colleagues:

> My first year teaching in middle school was horrible; she was my mentor but she was a tormentor. She constantly berated me and even complained to the principal about me. I could do nothing right, it was terrible and I found out she did this to others.

> One frustrating event occurred when a teacher went over my head and complained about me. I have a schedule that is constantly readjusted to suit the needs of students, but she said that I wasn't doing my job.

> I had a very negative experience early in my teaching career, and it has stayed with me. A fellow teacher disagreed with a decision that I made and she verbally assaulted me in front of the students; she then went to the administration.

SUMMARY

In this chapter we began by describing different types of peer consultation found in the professional literature; we also discussed teachers' perspectives of peer consultation that emerged from our study—a form of peer consultation characterized by a focus on fine-tuning teaching skills, reflective practice, and innovation. This chapter highlighted peer consultation skill #1, building healthy relationships by communicating, caring, and developing trust. We learned how peer consultants helped teachers by establishing and maintaining effective communication; taking a caring approach that positively affected teachers' satisfaction, sense of security, comfort, and classroom instruction; and building trust through nonthreatening, open conversations. In these ways peer consultants produced respectful, honest, dignified, and productive talk that was remarkable for its ease and naturalness. Chapter 3 presents our findings about peer consultation skill #2, using five guiding principles for structuring student learning experiences.

ACTIVITIES FOR TEACHERS AND ADMINISTRATORS

1. After a faculty meeting or discussion about school matters, take time to analyze your group's communication skills according to the seven types described in this chapter. Are your exchanges comfortable and productive? What can individuals and the group do to improve and to support mutual, reflective dialogue about teaching and learning?

2. Determine how actions teachers and administrators can engage to build trusting and caring interactions that enhance student learning as well as teacher learning.

3. Determine what opportunities teachers in your school have for nonthreatening, productive talk about their work. How might such opportunities be expanded?

SUGGESTED READING FOR FURTHER LEARNING

Developing Trust

Bryk, A. S., & Schneider, B. (2002). *Trust in schools: A core resource for improvement.* New York: Russell Sage.

Protocols: Examining Student Work Together

Blythe, T., Allen, D., & Powell, B. S. (1999). *Looking together at student work: A companion guide to "Assessing student learning."* New York: Teachers College Press.

Effective Communication

Schmuck, R. A., & Runkel, P. J. (1994). *The handbook of organizational development in schools and colleges* (4th ed.). Prospect Heights, IL: Waveland Press.

Caring in Schools

Beck, L. G. (1994). *Reclaiming educational administration as a caring profession.* New York: Teachers College Press.

Kochanek, J. R. (2005) *Building trust for better schools: Research-based practices.* Thousand Oaks, CA: Corwin Press.

Noddings, N. (1992). *The challenge to care in schools: An alternative approach to education.* New York: Teachers College Press.

Pellicer, L. O. (2003). *Caring enough to lead: Schools and the sacred trust.* Thousand Oaks, CA: Corwin Press.

3

Peer Consultation Skill #2: Using the Five Guiding Principles for Structuring Student Learning Experiences

Teachers know that there is much more to their knowledge than knowing the subject matter to be taught.

—Munby, Russell, & Martin, 2001, p. 900

My teacher neighbor who was going through national teacher certification helped me learn how important it is to be a facilitator and not just an instruction giver, how to think like a scientist.

—Elementary School Teacher

To the extent that you can open your students' eyes to wonder, you will be successful in the classroom.

—Middle School Teacher

Everyone wanted to be in his classes because they respected and admired his love of learning, which motivated learners. He was a great example for me.

—High School Teacher

This chapter opens with an examination of teachers' knowledge base, particularly their craft knowledge, a rapidly emerging research tradition. This is followed by a discussion of two powerful streams of research focusing on school improvement—the educational productivity research and the school effects research. The five guiding principles for structuring student learning experiences drawn from our study data are the centerpiece of this chapter.

TEACHERS' KNOWLEDGE BASE

What should teachers know to be effective in the classroom? Educational researchers have long investigated this question using multiple approaches. Through an examination of various research orientations and findings, we can more clearly see the breadth of knowledge teachers acquire and use in their teaching, as well as the extent to which they share this knowledge as peer consultants. We shall see, in fact, that teachers are adept at exploiting their knowledge base in the service of teaching and learning.

Historically, theoretical research orientations including positivism, interpretivism, and critically oriented approaches have been used to determine the professional knowledge base for teachers. Positivists stress the practical, empirical-analytical application of educational knowledge; interpretivists emphasize the *artistry* that operates in unique classes with unique students and attempt to understand how schools, classes, teachers, and students interact in society. In critically oriented approaches to research, knowledge about education is derived from analyzing the contradictions and shortcomings of educational and social institutions (Table 3.1) (see Tom and Valli [1990] for a thorough discussion of these approaches).

More recently, educational scholars have discussed a fourth research orientation, teachers' *craft* knowledge, as part of teachers' professional knowledge base. Although craft knowledge (i.e., systematic knowledge rooted in experience) is not based on the three major epistemological traditions noted earlier, it is considered the primary orientation of practicing teachers; teachers intuitively value it and recognize that "knowing" must include "knowing that" and "knowing how" (Munby et al., 2001, p. 885). Thus, craft knowledge is included here as the fourth research tradition in

Table 3.1 Research Traditions Used to Determine Teachers' Professional Knowledge Base

	Purpose	Beliefs	Nature of Research	Comment	Example
Positivism	To make statements about effectiveness of various practices (to develop a unified science of teaching, to improve teaching effectiveness)	• Establishes law-like generalizations. • Knowledge is cumulative. • Professional knowledge is separate from values. • Teachers can predict and control behavior. • Teachers should apply basic principles in a technical way. • Teachers act with will and purpose.	• Uses process-product research • Uses correlation/experimental study for causal claims about relationship of teacher behavior to student achievement	• The *rules* derived from such research are only hypotheses in the service of teachers' professional judgment. • The rules are only weak generalizations by which teacher can operate.	Studying the efficiency of using massed versus distributed practice for student learning
Interpretivism	To develop useful suggestions about the practice of teaching	• Meanings are local-specific and context-dependent. • Teachers construct meanings from educational and social encounters. • Values and facts are inseparable.	• Uses cases and interpretations • Seeks the meanings humans attach to the social, political, and cultural aspects of their lives • Attempts to understand character and culture • Uses theory (e.g., sociology, social science disciplines)	• Teachers use intuition, creativity, improvisation, expressions, judgment, sudden insight, and sensitivity. • Teachers analyze and clarify individual and cultural expressions and meanings, perceptions, assumptions, prejudgments, presuppositions.	• Studying ways we harm students and teachers • Studying conflicts between students and parents

	Purpose	Beliefs	Nature of Research	Comment	Example
Critically Oriented Approaches	• To place values at the heart of education • To achieve equality, justice, freedom, self-determination and other values in liberal, democratic traditions	• Values at center of inquiry; educational practice is overly technical, efficiency oriented, and neutrality oriented. • Humans can resist the pressure of dominant social or economic institutions. • Humans can transform institutions. • Complex aspects of teaching never before known or understood can and should be revealed. • Institutionalized education is sexist, racist, and class biased.	• Presumes a moral and political stance	Student is academically *left behind*, denied equality, justice, and freedom in education.	Studying whether textbook content is biased
Craft	To generate rules of practice out of knowledge derived from common sense, folklore, and experiences of practitioners and experts	• Teaching is a craft requiring technical skills, analytic knowledge, and the ability to apply knowledge to teaching. • Teacher education is an enterprise of traditionalism and apprentice training.	• Codifies practical experiences into maxims • Identifies practices of model teachers		Developing tips for teachers (e.g., "Never smile before Christmas," how to make transitions, how to deal with stress)

teachers' professional knowledge, although the nature of such knowledge has not been fully explored and is often ignored in teacher preparation programs.

What do we know about the nature of teachers' craft or experiential knowledge? We know that it is not comprised of abstract, isolated, discrete categories; rather, it is context dependent and embedded in practice (Borko & Putnam, 1996); it requires sensibility and reflectivity, and it represents "accumulated wisdom derived from teachers' and practice-oriented researchers' understandings of the meanings ascribed to the range of challenges (problems) inherent in teaching" (Grimmett & MacKinnon, 1992, p. 428). Experienced teachers possess a "wealth . . . [a] deep, sensitive . . . contextualized knowledge . . . [that grows out of] the wisdom of knowledge" (Leinhardt, 1993, pp. 18–19); they are clinicians who continually solve problems and make decisions. There is little doubt that the unknowable and indeterminate aspects of teaching often require a degree of artistry, and, in particular, creativity. Generally speaking, teachers possess vast amounts of pedagogical content knowledge and craft knowledge.

Good teachers are able to operate smoothly and efficiently in the classroom; consequently, because their extensive professional knowledge is imperceptible, it is easy to conclude that teaching skills are easily acquired. This is misleading; without a doubt, *learning to teach and to solve the myriad, complex problems of teaching are challenges of the first order; and this often necessitates working effectively with other teachers.* Our study demonstrates that peer consultants help colleague teachers create a bridge between knowledge and practice through practical reasoning and reflection (e.g., thinking and elaborating on thinking to connect it to practice). We also found that in teacher-to-teacher collaborative talk, the subtleties of teachers' knowledge were revealed and examined for merit and adaptation to the problems at hand.

What is the value of teacher-to-teacher collaborative talk? First, such talk fills a gap in teachers' professional development. Borko and Putnam (1996) described impediments to learning to teach, such as the quality of courses in the disciplines, lack of reflection in teacher education courses, poor student teaching opportunities, and beliefs and norms about teaching and learning that dominate student teaching settings. Such impediments contrast sharply with features of successful learning opportunities for teachers, which include assessing teachers' knowledge and beliefs about teaching, providing opportunities to deepen subject matter knowledge, treating teachers as learners, grounding teachers' learning and reflection on teaching in classroom practice, and providing time for reflection in collaborative relationships characterized by ongoing learning. We found that teacher-to-teacher talk produced such features; that is, peer consultants in our study routinely took into account the conditions of teaching and the perspectives of teachers, encouraged and modeled reflection, offered expertise and materials in relevant areas, and contextualized the problems under consideration.

THE EDUCATIONAL PRODUCTIVITY RESEARCH AND THE SCHOOL EFFECTS RESEARCH

Two strands of research findings comprise *the state-of-the-art empirical knowledge base in education:* The educational productivity research and the school effects research.

Strand #1: The Educational Productivity Research

The educational productivity research blends meta-analyses, content analyses, and expert ratings of studies to quantify the importance and consistency of variables that influence student learning (Fraser, Walberg, Welch, & Hattie, 1987; Reynolds, Wang, & Walberg, 1992; Walberg & Haertel, 1997; Wang, Haertel, & Walberg, 1990, 1993). This line of research has resulted in a six-factor model (Figure 3.1) that goes substantially beyond earlier models of school learning by including out-of-school influences such as social-psychological variables. These factors have been explicated in an emerging framework, along with models of adaptive instruction that describe knowledge about learning environments, effective schools, and other key variables related to learning. Broadly speaking, the educational productivity research demonstrates that proximal variables such as psychological, instructional, and home and community have more influence on learning than distal variables including demographic, policy, and organizational variables.

Strand #2: The School Effects Research

The second strand, the school effects research, is closely related to and overlaps with the productivity research; this strand of research combines school effectiveness studies and classic synthesis studies. From numerous meta-analyses of this research (i.e., research on school-, teacher-, and student-level variables that affect student achievement; Figure 3.2), Marzano (2000) concluded that student achievement is strongly influenced by attention to a specific set of factors and argued that such factors be used to inform staff development programs, evaluation, school improvement and reform efforts. In addition, Marzano (1998), Marzano, Gaddy, and Dean (2000); Marzano, Norford, Paynter, Pickering, and Gaddy (2001); and Marzano, Pickering, and Pollock (2001) described essential student abilities that could be enhanced by teaching strategies (Figure 3.3), instructional goals for classroom instruction (Figure 3.4), and teaching techniques relevant to these goals (Figure 3.5) (Marzano, 1998).

FROM KNOWLEDGE TO THE DEVELOPMENT OF A PROFESSIONAL LEARNING COMMUNITY

Our study data indicate that the actions of peer consultants, in their work with teachers, are consistent with findings from the aforementioned

Figure 3.1   Educational Productivity Research

Meta-analyses of research, content analyses, and expert ratings were used to quantify the importance and consistency of variables that influence learning.

Six categories influence school learning:

1. Student characteristics
2. Classroom practices
3. Home and community education contexts
4. Design and delivery of curriculum and instruction
5. School demographics, culture, climate, politics, and practices
6. State and district governance

Of 30 variables related to school learning:

The most impact on learning comes from proximal variables:

- Classroom management
- Student use of metacognitive strategies
- Student use of cognitive strategies
- Home environment and parental support
- Student and teacher social interaction

The weakest relationship to learning comes from distal variables:

- Program demographics
- School demographics
- State and district policies
- School policy and organization
- District demographics

Variables affecting learning, from the **Classroom Practices Category** (Wang et al., 1993):

- Classroom implementation support: efficient routines, rules, support
- Classroom instruction: clear and organized direct instruction
- Quantity of instruction: time on task
- Classroom assessment: frequent assessment
- Classroom management: questioning strategies, participation
- Student and teacher social interactions: positive student response to teacher and other students
- Student and teacher academic interactions: frequent calls for extended oral and written responses
- Classroom climate: shared interests, values, and cooperative goals

Variables affecting learning, from the **Design and Delivery of Curriculum and Instruction** Category (Wang et al., 1993):

- Program demographics: size of group: whole class, small group, one on one
- Curriculum and instruction: alignment among goals, content, instruction, assignments, evaluation
- Curriculum design: materials employ advance organizers

SOURCES: Fraser (1987); Reynolds, Wang, & Walberg (1992); Walberg & Hartel (1997); Wang, Haertel, & Walberg (1990; 1993).

Figure 3.2   Analysis and Interpretation of 30+ Years of Research on School
Effects Research

Reviews the literature on school-, teacher-, and student-level variables that affect student
achievement and translates it into principles educators can use to effect school reform. Includes
School Effectiveness Movement (Edmonds, 1979; Rutter, Maughan, Mortimer, & Ouston, 1979;
Klitgaard & Hall, 1975; and Brookover, Beady, Flood, Schweitzer, & Wisenbaker, 1979; Outlier
studies, Case studies, Implementation studies) and Classic Synthesis Studies (Bloom, 1984;
Walberg, 1980; Fraser, Walberg, Welch, & Hattie, 1987; Hattie, 1992; Wang, Haertel, & Walberg,
1993; Lipsey & Wilson, 1993; Cotton, 1995; Scheerens & Bosker, 1997; and Creemers, 1994).

Variables Influencing Student Achievement

School level variables (6.66% of the variance on achievement):

- Opportunity to learn
- Time
- Monitoring
- Pressure to achieve
- Parent involvement
- School climate
- Leadership
- Cooperation

Teacher level variables (13.34% of the variance on achievement):

- Instruction
- Curriculum design
- Classroom management

Student level variables (80% of the variance on achievement):

- Home atmosphere
- Prior knowledge
- Aptitude
- Interest

SOURCE: Adapted from Marzano (2000).

strands of research: Peer consultants' actions reflected empirical knowledge, craft knowledge derived from experience, empirically confirmed
craft knowledge including such matters as planning for an instructional
cycle (Figure 3.6), and relevant teaching models (Figure 3.7). This suggests
the importance of continued study of and comparisons across this knowledge base for school learning. *In our model of school-based academic leadership, we advocate the use of knowledge produced by both strands of research in
concert with craft knowledge and knowledge of shared instructional leadership*
(Blase & Blase, 2004a).

Text continues on p. 55

Figure 3.3   Student Abilities That Teaching Strategies Should Enhance

- Identifying similarities and differences
    Comparing
    Classifying
    Creating metaphors
    Creating analogies
- Summarizing and note taking
- Reinforcing effort and providing recognition
- Employing homework and practice
- Representing knowledge (nonlinguistic)
- Learning groups (cooperative learning)
- Setting objectives and providing feedback
- Generating and testing hypotheses
    Systems analysis
    Problem solving
    Decision making
    Historical investigation
    Experimental inquiry
    Invention
- Applying cues, questions, and advanced organizers
- Using specific types of knowledge
    Vocabulary
    Details
    Organizing ideas
    Skills and processes

SOURCE: Marzano, Gaddy, & Dean (2000); Marzano, Norford, Paynter, Pickering, & Gaddy (2001); Marzano, Pickering, & Pollock (2001).

Figure 3.4   Instructional Goals

At least three relatively straightforward implications about classroom instruction can be inferred from Marzano, Gaddy, and Dean's (2000) meta-analysis:

Implication #1: Teachers should identify knowledge and skills that are targets of instruction.

Implication #2: Teachers should identify and use specific instructional techniques for specific instructional goals.

Implication #3: Teachers should regularly use instructional techniques that apply to all types of instructional goals.

The constructs of the knowledge domains, cognitive system, metacognitive system, and self-system are organizers for the research on instruction. It is important for classroom teachers to be specific about the types of knowledge and processes that are to be the targets of classroom instruction so that specific instructional techniques can be used. Teachers should be able to answer the questions below relative to any unit of instruction in their classrooms.

What, if any, are my instructional goals relative to enhancing students' . . .

Figure 3.4 (Continued)

1. Knowledge Goals

Information:

- Understanding key vocabulary terms
- Understanding important details
- Understanding organizing ideas

Mental Processes:

- Ability to perform subject-specific algorithms
- Ability to perform subject-specific tactics
- Ability to perform subject-specific processes

Psychomotor Processes:

- Ability to perform subject-specific psychomotor skills

2. Cognitive Goals

Storage and Retrieval:

- Ability to store and retrieve knowledge

Basic Information Processing:

- Ability to identify similarities and differences
- Ability to represent knowledge in a variety of forms
- Ability to analyze the validity and reasonableness of new knowledge
- Ability to generate inferences using new knowledge
- Ability to apply conceptions, generalizations, and principles to new situations

Input/Output Processes:

- Ability to comprehend information presented orally
- Ability to comprehend information presented in written or symbolic terms
- Ability to communicate information in oral form
- Ability to communicate information in written or symbolic form

Knowledge Use:

- Ability to make decisions
- Ability to solve problems
- Ability to generate and test hypotheses using experimental inquiry
- Ability to investigate issues

3. Metacognitive Goals

- Ability to set explicit goals
- Ability to identify strategies to accomplish goals
- Ability to monitor progress toward goals
- Ability to monitor and control:
  - Accuracy and precision
  - Clarity
  - Impulsivity
  - Intensity of engagement
  - Focus

4. Self-Goals

- Understanding their beliefs about their personal attributes
- Understanding their beliefs about others
- Understanding their beliefs about how the world works
- Understanding their beliefs about purpose and what is important in life
- Understanding their beliefs about what can and cannot be changed and what they can and cannot do

SOURCE: Marzano, Gaddy, and Dean (2000).

Figure 3.5   Matching Teaching Techniques With Instructional Goals

Teachers should use specific instructional techniques for specific instructional goals.

Knowledge Goals

If the instructional goal is to enhance students' understanding of vocabulary terms and phrases:

- Provide students with a brief description or informal definition of each word or phrase.
- Have students describe the words or phrases in their own words and represent their personal descriptions using some form of nonlinguistic modality such as pictures, semantic maps, or charts.
- Occasionally have students review the terms and phrases making refinements in their representation.

If the instructional goal is to enhance students' understanding of details:

- Present the details in some form of story or elaborated description.
- Have students represent their understanding of the details in linguistic (notes, outlines) and nonlinguistic formats (pictures, semantic maps, charts, etc.).

If the instructional goal is to enhance students' understanding of organizing ideas such as concepts, generalizations, and principles:

- Demonstrate the organizing ideas to students in concrete terms.
- Have students apply the concept, generalization, or principle to new situations.

If the instructional goal is to enhance students' ability to perform subject-specific algorithms:

- Present the various steps in the algorithm.
- Have students practice the algorithm paying particular attention to how it might be improved.

If the instructional goal is to enhance students' ability to perform subject-specific tactics or processes:

- Present students with general rules or heuristics as opposed to specific steps.
- Have students practice the tactic or process paying particular attention to how it might be improved.

If the goal is to enhance students' ability to perform psychomotor skills:

- Present students with a model of the psychomotor skill.
- Have students practice the skill paying particular attention to how it might be improved.

Cognitive Goals

If the goal is to enhance students' ability to store and retrieve knowledge:

- Provide students with strategies that use the representation of knowledge in nonlinguistic forms such as mental images.

If the goal is to enhance students' ability to identify similarities and differences, to analyze the reasonableness of new knowledge, to generate inferences about new knowledge, or to apply organizing ideas:

- Provide students with a set of heuristics, as opposed to steps regarding the processes involved.
- Have students practice the heuristics, paying particular attention to how they might be improved.

If the goal is to enhance students' ability to represent knowledge in a variety of forms:

- Provide students with strategies for representing knowledge linguistically.
- Provide students with strategies for representing knowledge nonlinguistically.

If the goal is to enhance students' ability to comprehend information presented orally, such as by listening:

- Present students with a set of heuristics, as opposed to steps for the overall process of listening.
- Have students practice the heuristics, paying particular attention to how they might be improved.

If the goal is to enhance students' ability to comprehend information presented in written form:

- Provide students with information and strategies designed to enhance their ability to decode print. Have them practice the strategies, paying particular attention to how they might be improved.

Figure 3.5 (Continued)

- Provide students with a set of heuristics for the overall process of reading. Have students practice the heuristics, paying particular attention to how they might be improved.
- Provide students with strategies for activating what they know about a topic prior to reading.
- Provide students with strategies for summarizing information they have read.
- Provide students with information about the various text formats they will encounter.
- Provide students with strategies for representing what they have read in nonlinguistic form and as mental images.

If the goal is to enhance students' ability to present information in oral form, such as by speaking:

- Present students with information about the various conventions used in different situations.
- Provide students with heuristics for the overall process of speaking in various situations and have them practice the heuristics, paying particular attention to how they might be improved.
- Provide students with strategies for analyzing a topic in depth prior to speaking about it.

If the goal is to enhance students' ability to present information in written form:

- Provide students with heuristics for the overall process of writing and have students practice these heuristics, paying particular attention to how they might be improved.
- Present students with strategies for encoding thought into print.
- Present students with strategies for analyzing a topic in depth prior to writing about it.
- Provide students with information about the various discourse formats in which they will be expected to communicate.

If the goal is to enhance students' ability to make decisions, solve problems, or perform investigations:

- Provide students with heuristics for the overall processes of decision making, problem solving, and investigation and have them practice the heuristics, paying particular attention to how they might be improved.
- Provide students with strategies for using what they know about the topics that are the focus of problems, decisions, and investigations.

If the goal is to enhance students' ability to engage in experimental inquiry:

- Provide students with heuristics for the overall process of experimental inquiry and have them practice the heuristics, paying particular attention to how they might be improved.
- Provide students with strategies for generating and testing hypotheses.
- Have students apply the experimental inquiry process to a variety of situations.

Metacognitive Goals

If the goal is to enhance students' ability to set explicit goals, identify strategies for accomplishing goals or monitor progress toward goals:

- Have students verbalize their thinking as they engage in these functions, and analyze the effectiveness of their thought processes.
- Present students with information about the nature and importance of using the metacognitive system.

If the goal is to enhance students' ability to monitor their use of the various dispositions:

- Provide students with explicit information about the nature and function of the various dispositions.

Self Goals

If the goal is to enhance students' understanding of and control of their beliefs about self-attributes, self and others, the nature of the world, efficacy, or purpose:

- Have students verbalize their thinking relative to these areas.
- Have students make linkages between specific beliefs and specific behaviors in their lives.
- Have students identify those behaviors they wish to change.
- Provide students with strategies for altering their thinking relative to the behaviors they would like to change.

SOURCE: Marzano, Gaddy, and Dean (2000).

Figure 3.6

Step 1 Disaggregate data

Step 2 Develop timeline of skills, topics to be taught

Step 3 Deliver instructional focus

Step 4 Administer assessment

Step 5 Enrichment

Step 6 Tutorial

Step 7 Provide ongoing maintenance

Step 8 Monitoring

SOURCE: Brazosport Independent School District (2003).

Figure 3.7

Social Models

- Partners in learning
    Positive interdependence
    Structured inquiry
- Group investigation
- Role playing
- Jurisprudential inquiry

Development, Adaptation, and Instructional Design Models

- Conceptual systems theory
- Cognitive development
- Conditions of learning

Information-Processing Models

- Inductive thinking
- Concept attainment
- Mnemonics
- Advance organizers
- Scientific inquiry
- Inquiry training
- Synectics

Personal Models

- Nondirective teaching
- Enhancing self-esteem

Behavioral Models

- Mastery learning
- Direct instruction
- Simulation
- Social learning
- Programmed schedule

SOURCE: Joyce, Weil, & Calhoun (2000).

PEER CONSULTANTS' GUIDING PRINCIPLES FOR STRUCTURING LEARNING EXPERIENCES

The peer consultants described in our study exploited the teachers' knowledge base by deftly using the research findings of positivism, interpretivism, critically oriented research, and craft knowledge to help teachers understand the myriad aspects of teaching. Our data underscore the importance of five simple, yet effective, guiding principles (as listed in the following box) for structured student learning; these five principles reflect important aspects of the extant professional knowledge base in teaching. In short, what peer consultants consistently shared with teachers was the best of what we know about teaching and learning: *Naturally occurring facilitation among teachers yielded enlightened talk and action through informed experience.*

Furthermore, our findings point out that peer consultants demonstrate a meta-awareness of the complexities of teaching and local contexts. They did not have all the answers to complicated, perplexing instructional questions; rather, they capitalized on the authority of their experience to encourage other teachers to explore and experiment and to move from rigid, prescriptive teaching to emancipatory action to accommodate students' needs. Put differently, peer consultants presented numerous alternatives collected from classroom teaching experiences to help colleagues improve teaching; they modeled and taught empathy, flexibility, and reflection on classroom instruction and interaction with learners.

Five Guiding Principles for Structuring Learning Experiences

1. Address every child's needs.

2. Individualize and contextualize learning.

3. Engage students in cooperative learning.

4. Develop interdisciplinary approaches to learning.

5. Use technology in learning.

Guiding Principle #1: Address Every Child's Needs

All students' needs are different and they vary over time, regardless of their talents, disabilities, and demographics. That is, all people are *at risk, gifted, disabled, talented,* or *challenged* at different times; nowhere has this point been made clearer than in Capper, Frattura, and Keyes's (2000) groundbreaking book, *Meeting the Needs of Students of All Abilities.* These authors assert that "we are all alike" and "we are all unique" (p. 1). Their model of the teachers' role in meeting student needs suggests that teachers go beyond the typical inclusion approach; they must

> share responsibility with other teachers with expertise in a range of areas to support all students; create a proactive, preventative curriculum within school climates that ensure student success; work with educators who have a range of expertise to solve problems related to curriculum, school climate, and the social and behavioral aspects to meet the needs of students; collaboratively plan and teach with other members of the staff and community to meet the needs of all learners; and set a classroom climate that assumes expectations of peer support, wherein students understand their role is to be supportive for each other in academic, social, and behavioral areas. (Capper et al., 2000, p. 39)

Not surprisingly, our findings point out that peer consultants helped teachers to acknowledge and address diverse student needs:

> These words I have carried with me for years, and they continue to epitomize what I try to do as an educator: My favorite educator said, "Whoever walks into your classroom, be it a gifted student, average student, or wheelchair-bound student, you must make sure they know they are a valued member of your class and do your best to teach them." He was right.

> She taught me about different intelligences. Now I stop and think about how children learn and the different strategies that they can use to learn. I had been teaching to my strengths, not the strengths of the children; self-examination made me realize that. The student's needs should come first.

> I watched as a student with a learning disability who was unable to complete a project on time approached a teacher with obvious trepidation. The teacher, without incriminations, made a contract with the student for the project to be presented the following week. It was creative and inclusive and the student was never late again.

Guiding Principle #2: Individualize and Contextualize Learning

We found that peer consultants worked with teachers to help them individualize and contextualize instruction; they helped teachers select appropriate curricula, media, and technologies for learners, whatever their individual needs and current educational, social, and economic context.

Peer consultants were also deeply committed to helping teachers develop specific teaching practices that responded to a range of student differences:

> He taught me that you have to think like a teacher, take into account the age and level of your students, whether or not the activity you choose is appropriate and not just cute, and to consider the planning that is involved in preparing for the activity.

> This teacher once told me that she makes an individual educational plan for every student in her classroom. It made me more aware of the potential of individualized instruction. She planned for individuals as new units were entered, preassessments were given and each child had a plan to suit his point of need. Students were also challenged if they had shown mastery.

> I learned to let children select their own books and give them time, as much time as they need, to practice. This is one way to individualize a reading program for students from different contexts without having five reading groups.

> She helped me design a rubric to develop multi-level lessons that accommodate student groupings. It can be a daunting task to deal with different functioning levels of students in one class; you always feel like you are chasing your tail and doing only a so-so job, but the rubric helps.

We learned that peer consultants also encouraged and taught teachers to use multiple approaches and methods in their teaching. Peer consultants bridged theory and practice by expanding teachers' repertoires, thereby enabling teachers to respond creatively to various learning and thinking styles as well as multiple intelligences (for a synthesis of key related research, see Gregory, 2005; Gregory & Chapman, 2005).

> I learned there are "many arrows for a single target."

> I learned how to reduce group size to accommodate readers; this also enables me to read more one-on-one with the students. Now I use different-leveled books for reading with students.

> Because of the students' learning style, this teacher heavily used overheads to illustrate and reinforce.

> The teacher combined verbal and written skills in a social studies class on the period of reconstruction. She had her class go over the Jim Crow Laws and choose one to present to their classmates, followed by designing a political cartoon demonstrating the law.

Tips offered by peer consultants about planning, student initiative in classroom activities, and reflection helped teachers work effectively and efficiently with many different students:

> I learned that teaching in a vacuum is a flawed strategy; that one has to coordinate their resources and take into account environmental elements and get them stabilized.

> He helped me help the students to be self-regulated and he helped me to teach them test-taking skills.

> I told [my peer consultant] about a teacher who did not give the students any choices, and she helped me see not only that it was a dictatorship, but also that it constrained students' learning and responsibility.

> He taught me to reflect after the lesson about my students' individual progress and use this to plan for future lessons.

With regard to special education, Kauffman and Hallahan (2005) explain:

> Although good general education is demanding, special education requires greater control and precision along several dimensions of instruction: pacing or rate, intensity, relentlessness, structure, reinforcement, pupil to teacher ratio, curriculum, and monitoring or assessment. Because all of these dimensions of teaching are continuous distributions (can vary from a little to a lot), education can differ in the degree of specialness. Ultimately, special education is only worthwhile if it means special instruction for learners at the extremes of the distribution of performance. (p. 55)

Accordingly, teachers in our study reported numerous ways their peer consultants helped them to extend, remediate, and adjust instruction for exceptional children who have difficulty hearing, seeing, speaking, moving, thinking, learning, focusing, and controlling emotions and behavior as well as for talented and gifted children:

> He taught me that gifted is not so much in the teaching, but is more in the results the student produces.

> She achieves miracles as she instructs students who "couldn't make it." Her strategy is to individualize the instruction to each student's level and to hold students accountable for their best. She

is tireless in her faith about what can occur; I have that faith now, too.

A math teacher recommended a particular way to teach the facts to students who are behind, starting with square numbers and then branching out. I thought it was a very strange idea; however, I have incorporated it and I have found it to be helpful. It reinforces the concept of areas, square numbers, and square roots in addition to helping students learn to master facts.

She showed me how to use Christmas lights in instruction with visually impaired students and how to make many items by hand. I plan to continue to pick her brain, and it will, in turn, benefit classroom teaching as I work with other teachers about their instruction.

Guiding Principle #3: Engage Students in Cooperative Learning

We found that peer consultants often encouraged teachers to use cooperative learning, an instructional technique which, according to the research, has been consistently linked to positive effects on student learning; in fact, evidence about students helping each other has indicated a high effect size (i.e., students learn more), a finding that should not be ignored (Walberg & Haertel, 1997). By learning together, students become aware and appreciative of individual differences and cultural diversity, and such interdependence fosters a more supportive and comfortable climate in classrooms and schools. Cooperative learning, on average, increases achievement and motivation; extends thinking skills; increases conflict resolution; and improves social, interpersonal, and leadership skills as well as attitudes toward school; it also increases self-confidence and self-esteem (Walberg & Haertel, 1997):

She did a professional development session on cooperative learning—the basics: how to put kids into groups and why. Then she told me how her small group setting worked and discussed it with me in great depth. I decided to try it—with her help—and I found it to be more effective.

She has her students directly involved in their learning by creating activities around the curriculum with her. This flip-flopped the notion of teacher-made and teacher-directed, results-oriented activities for me.

She shared some research on effective cooperative learning strategies that she had gotten in her graduate classes; I had been skeptical, but I have tried it since and it is effective.

I learned about it [cooperative learning] from this maverick teacher whose main concern was that learning take place within her classroom. She showed me that cooperative groups and journals were very helpful.

I learned how to use peer tutoring when I have kids who are not getting a concept after trying several different ways of teaching it to them. Often kids can explain it so other kids get it. This is also helpful to you and other kids.

She shared with me her expertise in paired reading, which I had not learned before. In paired reading, one of the readers is considered a struggling reader. She added her own additional idea, a different way of thinking about a situation I was teaching about.

Moreover, peer consultants offered teachers suggestions about cooperative planning, studying, and behavior management:

I learned to have groups of students plan, prepare, and present chapter outlines for students to fill in when they are reviewing for the year.

She showed me how to do an excellent review for students by having students put their ID number instead of their names on quizzes and then distributing the quizzes to let students discuss the answers.

He used group competition to help students learn and group work to study for a test and help each other achieve for the good of the whole group.

She taught me a self-management strategy through which students monitor themselves and stay accountable. It also helps with their behavior because when they are on task they are usually behaving.

Our study also revealed that peer consultants helped teachers integrate *learning center* strategies with cooperative learning approaches:

I learned from this teacher how to use centers. What a thrill! Each center focuses on a different objective and the kids rotate through the centers. They frequently help each other learn at the centers.

He showed me everything about learning centers, and he made me realize that centers are not only for lower school students.

She showed me how to incorporate the learning center idea into my daily classroom instruction.

Guiding Principle #4: Develop Interdisciplinary Approaches to Learning

In the past decade, there has been a proliferation of comparative studies, case studies, action research reports, and research reviews focusing on multidisciplinary, integrated, interdisciplinary approaches to curriculum (i.e., beyond the separate-subject approach). Reviews of research indicate that, despite difficulties associated with sustaining such a curriculum, students do as well or better on standard measures of academic achievement as the curriculum becomes more interdisciplinary and integrated; specifically, such a curriculum enables students to see connections between ideas from different disciplines. The kind and degree of collegial support for efforts of this nature are crucial to students' success (Beane & Brodhagen, 2001). Not surprisingly, we discovered that peer consultants consistently provided appropriate support for teachers:

Integrating instruction sounds good, but it was only after I was able to see it in action and in a teacher's classroom that it hit home with me. I saw how it could be done and why it is so brain compatible.

He taught me how to collaboratively plan interdisciplinary units with my team. I learned to incorporate class group readings and vocabulary lists into my classes. The kids even work on the rules through reading comprehension exercises.

This teacher taught me how to use music to teach various concepts such as sequencing, remembering how to spell, and phonics rules. I learned to introduce addition and subtraction through story problems, we use gummy bears and talk through the learning, then the students are allowed to eat the ones we subtracted (took away). It is a fun way to introduce the concepts.

This teacher was teaching basic reading and we realized that students in my social studies classes not only wanted to attend her class, but needed to learn social studies as they were learning to read as well.

I learned how to provide a five-minute mini-lesson from horticulture to practice a math or English skill.

This teacher showed me how to incorporate music into much of my special students' day. Through music and rhythm they were able to learn different subjects using different modalities. Movement activities were based on brain-based learning research as well.

I learned how to use mnemonics for learning the steps of division.

Guiding Principle #5: Use Technology in Learning

The use of technologies in schools has increased exponentially in recent decades and now includes computers and communications technologies such as computer networks; needless to say, the current, most advanced technology available for teaching and learning should be considered *educational technology*. Computer technology, for example, has been used in classrooms for tutorial learning, exploratory learning, *learning by doing*, and communication such as electronic mail, file transfers, retrieval and sharing of information from the World Wide Web, and collaborative discussion and learning. Most importantly, computer technology has been shown to have significant effects on learning (Walberg & Haertel, 1997).

To be sure, teachers should not simply use computers in classroom instruction to more efficiently provide drill and practice (where students learn the same thing as they would in class, but faster); teachers must understand successful applications of computer technology to improve instruction, and, in particular, to help students perform increasingly complex thinking and problem solving. This requires ongoing opportunities for teachers to design new instructional strategies and new learning objectives for students. Sadly, research indicates that teachers seldom have such opportunities (Schwab & Foa, 2001).

Our study data indicated that peer consultants helped teachers, at least minimally, to design and adapt computer instruction for their classrooms. Teachers disclosed that their peer consultants helped them learn about the use of technology for direct classroom instruction as well as for various administrative needs such as grading:

Everyone was expected to use the grading software, yet there were no manuals or literature for learning it. This teacher taught me how to use the software in the computer and helped me realize many applications that I probably would not have noticed if I had just begun to explore and use it on my own.

He took his planning time to sit down with me and show me how to use computers and various other technologies in order to be innovative in my instruction.

She carefully explained the components, benefits, and limitations of a computer-based math program and made herself available for any and all of my questions.

She helped me catch up with the new developments in technology since I came out of college. She showed me how to use computers for student writing.

He showed me how to use digital pictures in various ways.

She demonstrated how to incorporate technology into the social studies classroom.

SUMMARY

This chapter began with a discussion of a fourth research tradition and knowledge base: teachers' knowledge base. We argued that this type of knowledge should be an important part of teachers' professional knowledge base; we also demonstrated that peer consultants helped teachers create a bridge between such knowledge and practice. We described the two most respected strands of empirical knowledge that focus on school improvement: the educational productivity research and the school effects research. We noted that the peer consultants described in our study helped teachers improve teaching in ways consistent with this research. The heart of this chapter describes peer consultation skill #5, exploiting the knowledge base. Here, we described the five effective guiding principles for structured learning experiences taught by peer consultants to help teachers address every child's needs, individualize and contextualize learning, engage students in cooperative learning, develop interdisciplinary approaches to learning, and use technology to improve classroom instruction and student learning. Chapter 4 focuses on peer consultation skill #3: planning and organizing for learning.

IMPLICATIONS FOR PRACTICE

1. Teachers should use both empirical and craft knowledge to inform teacher-to-teacher talk and action.

2. Educational leaders should facilitate the naturally occurring teacher talk in their schools; this, in turn, will help teachers work with diverse students, address individual student needs, use cooperative

learning, develop interdisciplinary approaches to learning, and use technology for instructional purposes.

3. Teachers should integrate professional knowledge with their colleagues' contextually informed craft knowledge. This integration should be reflectively examined and adapted to the instructional problems under consideration.

4. Teachers should actively lobby administrators for more opportunities and make use of them for teaching and learning.

SUGGESTED READING FOR FURTHER LEARNING

The Educational Productivity and School Effects Research

Marzano, R. J. (1998). *A theory-based meta-analysis of research on instruction.* Aurora, CO: Mid-continent Research for Education and Learning.

Marzano, R. J. (2000). *A new era of school reform: Going where the research takes us.* Aurora, CO: Mid-continent Research for Education and Learning.

Marzano, R. J., Gaddy, B. B., & Dean, C. (2000). *What works in classroom instruction.* Aurora, CO: Mid-continent Research for Education and Learning.

Marzano, R. J., Norford, J. S., Paynter, D. E., Pickering, D. J., & Gaddy, B. B. (2001). *A handbook for classroom instruction that works.* Alexandria, VA: Association for Supervision and Curriculum Development.

Marzano, R. J., Pickering, D. J., & Pollock, J. E. (2001). *Classroom instruction that works: Research-based strategies for increasing student achievement.* Alexandria, VA: Association for Supervision and Curriculum Development.

Marzano, R. J., Waters, T., & McNulty, B. A. (2005). *School leadership that works: From research to results.* Alexandria, VA: Association for Supervision and Curriculum Development.

Addressing Every Child's Needs

Capper, C. A., Frattura, E., Keyes, M. W. (2000). *Meeting the needs of students of all abilities.* Thousand Oaks, CA: Corwin Press.

Chapman, C., & King, R. (2003). *Differentiated instructional strategies for reading in the content areas.* Thousand Oaks, CA: Corwin Press.

Chapman, C., & King, R. (2005). Differentiated assessment strategies. Thousand Oaks, CA: Corwin Press.

Ferguson, D., Droege, C., Guojóbsdóttir, H., Lester, J., Meyer, G., Ralph, G., et al. (2001). *Designing personalized learning for every student*. Alexandria, VA: Association for Supervision and Curriculum Development.

Gore, M. C. (2004). *Successful inclusion strategies for secondary and middle school teachers: Keys to help struggling learners access the curriculum*. Thousand Oaks, CA: Corwin Press.

Gregory, G. H. (2005). *Differentiating instruction with style*. Thousand Oaks, CA: Corwin Press.

Gregory, G. H., & Kuzmich, L. (Eds.). (2004). *Data driven differentiation in the standards-based classroom*. Thousand Oaks, CA: Corwin Press.

Karten, T. (2005). *Inclusion strategies that work! Research-based methods for the classroom*. Thousand Oaks, CA: Corwin Press.

Sprenger, M. (2003). *Differentiated through learning styles and memory*. Thousand Oaks, CA: Corwin Press.

Stone, R. (2004). *Best teaching practices for reaching all learners*. Thousand Oaks, CA: Corwin Press.

Tomlinson, C. A. (2003). *Fulfilling the promise of the differentiated classroom: Strategies and tools for responsive teaching*. Alexandria, VA: Association for Supervision and Curriculum Development.

Cooperative Learning

Jacobs, G. M., Power, M. A., & Inn, L. W. (Eds.). (2002). *The teacher's source-book for cooperative learning: Practical techniques, basic principles, and frequently asked questions*. Thousand Oaks, CA: Corwin Press.

Johnson, D. W., Johnson, R. T., & Holubec, E. J. (1994). *Cooperative learning in the classroom*. Alexandria, VA: Association for Supervision and Curriculum Development.

Marlowe, B., & Page, M. L. (Eds.). (2005). *Creating and sustaining the constructivist classroom*. Thousand Oaks, CA: Corwin Press.

Interdisciplinary Approaches to Learning

Drake, S. (1998). *Creating integrated curriculum: Proven ways to increase student learning*. Alexandria, VA: Association for Supervision and Curriculum Development.

Drake, S. M., & Burns, R. C. (2004). *Meeting standards through integrated curriculum*. Alexandria, VA: Association for Supervision and Curriculum Development.

Exline, J. (2005). *Integrating inquiry across the curriculum*. Alexandria, VA: Association for Supervision and Curriculum Development.

Jacobs, H. H. (1997). *Mapping the big picture: Integrating curriculum & assessment K–12*. Alexandria, VA: Association for Supervision and Curriculum Development.

Technology in Learning

Bray, M., Brown, A., & Green, T. (Eds.) (2004). *Technology and the diverse learner.* Thousand Oaks, CA: Corwin Press.

Jukes, I., Dosaj, A., & Macdonald, B. (Eds.) (2000). *NetSavvy.* Thousand Oaks, CA: Corwin Press.

Ormiston, M. J. (2004). *Conquering InfoClutter: Timesaving technology solutions for teachers.* Thousand Oaks, CA: Corwin Press.

Pflaum, W. D. (2004). *The technology fix: The promise and reality of computers in our schools.* Alexandria VA: Association for Supervision and Curriculum Development.

Staudt, C. (2005). *Changing how we teach and learn with handheld computers.* Thousand Oaks, CA: Corwin Press.

4

Peer Consultation Skill #3: Planning and Organizing for Learning

She helped me organize my lessons—what to teach, when to teach it, when to test, and what materials to use.

She taught me how to do team planning, differentiated units, and inter-disciplinary curriculum as well as thematic units.

We begin this chapter with a brief review of significant research on teachers' professional development. This is followed by findings from our study of peer consultants' planning and organizing skills related to student learning, the essential core skill for teaching effectiveness. It is a skill set that consists of three dimensions: metathemes of planning, getting organized for instruction, and lesson planning. We also share our findings about the dark side of planning.

TEACHERS' PROFESSIONAL DEVELOPMENT

More than three decades ago, Judith Warren Little (1982) studied how teachers learn on the job; she found that collaboration and reflective collegial dialogue among teachers were critical to professional learning and school success. From her study, Little identified four critical practices necessary for teachers' ongoing professional growth and development:

1. Teachers engage in frequent, continuous, and increasingly concrete and precise talk about teaching practice.

2. Teachers are frequently observed and provided with useful critiques of their teaching.

3. Teachers plan, design, research, evaluate, and prepare teaching materials together.

4. Teachers teach each other the practice of teaching. (pp. 331–332)

These four practices were evident in our study as teachers described naturally occurring professional conversations with peer consultants. Apparently, collegial work remains vital to teachers' growth, and, as described earlier, such growth culminates in improved instruction and student learning.

Recently, Stroot and colleagues (1999) studied new teachers' (i.e., first-year and new-to-the-school teachers) perceived needs and the impact of a mentoring program designed to help them address those needs. These researchers found that new teachers benefited in nine identified areas with the help of mentors:

1. managing the classroom,

2. creating expectations of self as a teacher,

3. obtaining resources and materials,

4. assessing students,

5. motivating students,

6. identifying effective teaching methods,

7. responding to individual student needs,

8. communicating with colleagues, and

9. communicating with parents.

In one other area—planning and organizing time and work—new teachers' needs were not met. Although the peer consultants in our study were not formally designated as mentors, the teachers with whom they worked reported similar areas of growth and need. We found that peer consultants helped teachers improve practice; their dialogue with teachers comprised "an exploration by peers of complex issues in creative ways" (McBride & Skau, 1995, p. 273).

Relatedly, Evertson and Smithey (2000) found that teachers who engaged in discussions with trained mentors were more effective than others at planning and organizing for teaching (e.g., implementing and maintaining discipline and class routines, managing instruction, obtaining cooperation from students, and keeping students on task). Kohler, Crilley, Shearer, and Good (1997) found that changes implemented by teachers based on collegial dialogue (about direct instruction and reciprocal learning strategies for students) were significant and permanent; however, they further noted that when modifications were not discussed with teachers, implementation was less likely. Before beginning our study we wondered if peer consultants, in their work with teachers, achieved similar results, particularly with regard to planning and organizing for teaching. Our findings confirmed that this was, indeed, the case: Peer consultation is directly linked to practical improvements in planning and organizing for classroom instruction.

In the remainder of this chapter, we describe conversations between peer consultants and teachers that centered on planning and organizing for instruction, the essential, technical core skill for teaching effectiveness. The primary elements of planning and organizing for instruction that appeared in our data are

- metathemes of planning,
- getting organized for instruction, and
- elements of lesson planning.

It is important to mention that all elements represented in these particular findings are comparable to those discussed in the previous chapters for the high-profile productivity and school effects research.

METATHEMES OF PLANNING

Our findings show that peer consultants frequently shared with teachers the essence of good instructional planning—the metathemes—including *defining and achieving goals, maintaining high expectations, developing critical thinking skills,* and *motivating students* with lessons typified by student choice and discovery. In addition, peer consultants and teachers often *planned together or demonstrated planning strategies* for each other.

Defining and Achieving Goals

From peer consultants, teachers learned how to define goals, adjust them to student needs, and integrate them with reflective learning activities:

He taught me to develop a long-term goal and that it was the goal as well as the process of reaching the goal that was important. He also taught me that the child needs to know the long-term goal as well as what is expected.

She gave me my initial introduction to the concepts of learning styles, cognitive style, multiple intelligences, and brain-based learning. Now I use the knowledge about student learning and cognitive styles as I plan and carry out instruction. Through this independent reading and study, my teaching has continued to be infused with new ideas and I continue to refine my strategies for adapting instruction to student needs. By far this was the most influential strategy I learned in recent years.

Reflecting and planning go hand-in-hand. She taught me how to ask the right questions of myself before and after a lesson so the lesson could be improved or so I could assess the children fairly. Now I am a really reflective teacher, and it isn't that hard to reflect before, during, or after a lesson. I could reflect on reflecting if I had to.

Maintaining High Expectations and Developing Critical Thinking Skills

Acknowledging the diversity of student needs and abilities, the peer consultants in our study encouraged teachers to maintain high but reasonable expectations:

He told me to teach to the group that I have. I change my teaching regarding the number of objectives and breadth of curriculum that I expect the children to cover. My classes are heterogeneous, so this includes special needs, average, and gifted students.

A teacher I worked with expressed her opinion that the current group of ninth graders had been coddled and told "good try" for too long. She taught me how to make them responsible and accountable for their learning because we live in an outcome-based society and good try won't cut it.

Peer consultants also emphasized encouraging students to think critically:

I learned to engage the students in reflective thinking to look at what worked and what didn't work and to help them try to build mental schema. My peer taught me a technique for physics lab whereby the students have a focus on inductive thinking and problem solving after they collect data. I had never encountered this approach before. Students were able to think inductively and to generate many of the foundational formulas used in physics.

He taught me to periodically say there is no dumb question and other similar phrases to encourage students. Many students don't grasp new concepts quickly or they do not have the courage to ask questions. I watched how he conducted class discussions. Opinions were encouraged but he always gently prodded students' to back up their opinions with facts or evidence. He never let the discussion turn into simply a gathering of opinions or soapbox talk.

Motivating Students With Lessons Involving Student Choice and Discovery

Peer consultants helped teachers implement motivating lessons in ways consistent with research on student motivation, student interest, student success, and classroom climate; and this contributed to the development of a learning community in the classroom:

Now I try to connect everything I am teaching to their lives and show them how they will use this skill or information in the future. Sometimes when I have trouble tying the knowledge to their lives and their futures, I make up stories to make it feel authentic.

I use this teacher's strategy of getting students actively involved in the writing process, making a rough draft, getting peers' responses formally and informally, revising, editing, and writing new drafts.

She discussed strategies for motivating uninterested students like varying delivery, hands-on activities, incorporating art into history, and current events exercises.

I learned to allow students to do almost any kind of project, a portfolio, writing, paper, or action research or video, literally anything to demonstrate their learning.

She gave the students a variety of activities from which to choose to complete as their required task. These activities suited a multitude of learning styles and the kids loved it; they felt empowered, worked harder, and their scores improved.

I thought it was crazy to allow my students to give input on instruction, but he told me how to allow them to tell me what they wanted to learn, how to plan my lessons accordingly and how to allow them to come up with questions that were fair.

Moreover, our data indicate that peer consultants helped teachers learn the importance of creating a supportive classroom climate to motivate students:

> The room needs to be beautiful and well decorated, have extra touches. Now when the students are doing individual or small group work, I play some music, and Miles Davis's *Kind of Blue* is a favorite of mine.

> He taught me to express things positively, a test is an opportunity, you get to come to class instead of you have to come to class. It helps me think of life in positive terms and the students and I smiled more. It lightens our mood.

> I feel like it is sometimes great for students not to be scared about doing the correct thing all the time. In drama class, for example, there isn't much pressure on students to always do it right; it is fun and it builds creativity; it allows spontaneity and kids are more like themselves. I learned that the class should be like a community.

PLANNING TOGETHER

Finally, peer consultants went beyond the metathemes of planning to actively demonstrate planning strategies or directly plan lessons with teachers:

> She demonstrated what works for her in special activities and lesson planning. This has always made me feel very good because she has shown concern, time, and caring for me, professionally and personally.

> Planning with this teacher helps me create quality lessons. It is nice to bounce ideas off of her and get additional ideas and activities. She helps me think through the steps I want to take with each lesson and gives me ideas about what will and will not work. My lessons are now more successful because I have incorporated someone else's opinions.

According to our data, collaborative planning increased teachers' confidence.

> We noticed things in each other's approach that work, and we try to incorporate the strategies that are new or that work for a particular

project. It is great to feel more confident about how you view student work.

This teacher and I swapped ideas and communicate with one another about lesson plans. I have used her as a model for my teaching philosophy. She has made me think more to the point on the topic and made me think about how to use students' thinking skills. It has opened my planning up. This gives me confidence in myself. She has opened up the other side of teaching for me and made me realize that I should try and do more for more students, other than the students who take my class; basically try and touch everyone.

A colleague and friend assured me early in my teaching career that mistakes are going to happen . . . and it is all right to admit the error and correct it. She said that one of the greatest fears of teachers is that . . . students will lose respect for them and laugh; actually students will respect you for not thinking you are infallible and they will laugh with you rather than at you if you can laugh at yourself.

Teachers also discussed cooperative planning in relation to increased creativity, including *out-of-the-box* thinking:

The teacher was very knowledgeable about the subject and helped me plan effective activities. My thinking is now more out of the box. I am more open to trying things and I feel supported.

I plan with another teacher who teaches the same subject; it helps generate more creative ideas. Now I am more relaxed and I know more about the subject from studying with my buddy. I am also less stressed when approaching new units.

Together we come up with great new ideas, in other words we tag team; we build upon each other's ideas. If something isn't effective, we review our methods. I feel empowered to be the best for the students.

GETTING ORGANIZED FOR INSTRUCTION

Getting organized was the second critical element of planning and organizing for instruction revealed in our study. We found that peer consultants helped teachers with *fundamental, technical organization to streamline routine tasks and procedures:*

One of my friends, a teacher in the department, taught me how to organize my materials. I had found it hard to organize in folders the way my previous supervising teacher had taught me. I couldn't keep up with stuff, I couldn't locate things. My friend gave me a better strategy. She even used Tupperware containers to separate out supplies. It was very logical and doing that helped me to keep one step ahead of my class preparations. It was easier to take materials up and to pass them out and to give different materials to groups doing different things; it saved time.

A teacher taught me how to be organized and stay on track. She told me to keep a daily agenda, to not spend too much time on a particular section, to break the class into sections, and to use different methods.

She truly has a place for everything and everything in its place. She files everything immediately, writes everything down, labels everything, and she keeps her students informed of where everything is.

A teacher gave me tips on time management and how to handle the paperwork. I learned that planning actually requires thought—that I should plan ahead so I wouldn't be playing catch up.

Peer consultants frequently linked being well organized and being an effective, caring teacher:

He was such a caring teacher; and all of his students walked away from his class realizing that the attitude of the teacher, no matter what level, goes a long way. He was also well prepared and organized and wasted no class time. I now want to make sure that every minute counts in my classroom as a result of time spent in his class. He modeled what he taught.

Last, we found that peer consultants helped teachers see the relationship between classroom organization and student responsibility:

I watched him teach and learned how to let students assist with various tasks. Normally I controlled everything, but I have now learned to allow students to pass out or take up materials, help clean up and do other tasks.

ELEMENTS OF LESSON PLANNING

Peer consultants viewed lesson planning as crucial to effective planning and organizing for instruction. Teachers shared accounts of peer consultants' general approaches to lesson planning:

My mentor actually asked me what my objective was when I was about to do a lesson. It wasn't clear and I wasn't teaching what I thought. She helped me become more focused and to clarify my objectives. When I returned to teaching after getting my youngest child into school, this lady helped me condense my time and organize my lesson plans so that I would be highly effective as a teacher but still be able to be a mother and wife. Her students and colleagues knew that she would do whatever was needed but would do it in a timely, uncomplicated way. She was never stressed by things hanging over her because of that.

When I first began teaching, I tended to go too fast and thus would end up losing my kids' attention. This veteran teacher praised my teaching but helped me to slow down so I would be more effective. I was having trouble figuring out how much time activities and lessons would actually take in class. I would plan what I thought was the correct amount, but I would be finished well before the end of the period, standing in front of the group with nothing left to do. It is frightening and confusing. My neighbor teacher's advice was to plan one-and-a-half times as much work as I expected to accomplish. She also said to consciously slow down, not to panic, and to believe that pacing would come with experience. She told me to stay flexible to try to listen to the students' responses during the lesson and to try to access them during the lesson.

It was also evident that teachers learned much from their peer consultants about evaluation of students:

The teachers on our grade level met as a team to evaluate writing stages of students' papers. We shared feedback with each other and we explained our reasons for placing students at a certain stage.

One of the teachers on our team helped us organize all of our student data and shared responsibility for it. It relieved us of a lot of paperwork. She showed me that grading notebooks twice a semester was more efficient and promoted student responsibility rather than checking assignments every day.

One teacher helped me learn how to use rubrics for grading projects and writing.

TEACHER TIPS

Our study data contained countless *tips* about many aspects of lesson planning teachers learned from peer consultants:

⭐ Tip: State Objectives

I learned to give students a focus at the beginning of each class so they knew what their goal was each day.

I learned how to put the objective on the board and make it clear. Now I put the schedule on the board and it helps the students plan.

⭐ Tip: Divide Learning Into Steps

I learned from another teacher how to develop outcome-based goals supported by incremental learning steps.

I learned about an umbrella tool that helps me structure lessons and generate subobjectives.

⭐ Tip: Attend to Student Readiness

I was told to have every student's attention before beginning my teaching. I was taught how to do a body check: Are you sitting on your spot, hands on your lap, quietly, ready to learn?

⭐ Tip: Use Advance Organizers

This teacher showed me how to have students keep a table of contents in the front of their notebooks with all assignments, notes, and so on. Students number everything to correspond with the table of contents. It helps them stay organized.

This teacher showed me how to build a weekly organizer—a table of contents—and maintain it in the classroom as a visual representation of the assignments for that week.

I learned to use visual organizers, particularly at the outset of a lesson.

⭐ Tip: Access Prior Learning

Now I talk about prior knowledge and experiences, I ask the children if the story reminded them of anything, so they can connect it with a real-life situation, this keeps them with the topic.

Tips identified in our data dealt with maintaining lesson flow to achieve objectives designed during planning. They include the following:

⭐ Tip: Move Around

I learned how to move a lot in class. A negative example was the teacher who sat behind her desk and spoke to her students only through a microphone during almost every class period.

⭐ Tip: Allow Wait Time and Encourage Student Participation

She taught me how to facilitate learning through the use of wait-time, avoiding being the center and all-knowing figure, teaching students to listen and value their peers' comments, to not repeat student answers—that is, insist students speak loud enough for all to hear.

I learned the strategy of increasing the amount of time I gave each student to respond. Now I ask the question and then stop talking, I don't paraphrase. I know that it can be confusing for children to try to answer my question while trying to listen to me at the same time.

She kept them engaged and she asked wonderful questions. I wanted such questions to come from my mouth as well when I taught. It was a real high point in my learning about teaching.

⭐ Tip: Model Learning for Students

I learned to use sample papers from other classes with names removed to show students what is considered excellent.

This teacher explained her objective and then always modeled what she wanted students to do.

⭐ Tip: Reinforce Learning

She explained several times, then she had several students repeat what she had explained. I realize it is very important to reinforce their learning.

He taught me the difference between memorizing information and getting information into the long-term memories of students.

⭐ Tip: Give Good Directions and Ask Advanced-Level Questions

She said, "Talk so their ears will listen." So now I preteach, give clear instructions in a multisensory format and give clear directions.

He asked me lots of questions to help me construct my own knowledge of a given subject. He challenged me to teach with the basic information and then to proceed to ask questions that made students apply their knowledge.

THE DARK SIDE OF PLANNING AND ORGANIZING FOR LEARNING

Although teachers in our study learned much about effective planning and organizing for learning from peer consultants, they also shared stories about ineffective planning and disorganization by other teachers; witnessing such poor modeling evoked strong feelings in our respondents and clearly reinforced the need to plan and organize well:

This teacher became frustrated when a student asked why. She said "You're getting the right answer, don't worry about it; girls don't need to understand math." The student then hated math. Now when I teach, I always begin with why we need to know the particular skill. I go out of my way to reach all students regardless of gender and to help students learn that there are different ways to solve math problems.

I know this teacher who lectures all the time, never does any activities or labs, and the students are completely bored and unfocused; they got very little from the class and I think they began to hate the subject from what I could tell by talking with them later. She was very intent on constantly giving notes, very detailed notes. She hated to sway from the routine unless it was lab day. I knew the kids hated it and this fact influenced my teaching for the better.

I have seen teachers use nothing but overheads and note-taking methods. All the students learn is how to memorize. It is a boring and useless class with no life and no excitement.

This teacher had students diagram sentences for ten straight weeks; every day, it was done on handouts and homework was more handouts—drill and kill.

This teacher asked the former student's sister if he was in jail yet. She was embarrassed, but mostly noted the teacher's dictator-like style and tendency to humiliate her students.

SUMMARY

This chapter has described peer consultation skill # 3, planning and organizing for instruction, the core skill for improving teaching effectiveness. Specifically, we discussed the three major aspects of planning and organizing drawn from our study. First, we described the metathemes of planning (i.e., determining and achieving goals, maintaining high expectations and developing critical thinking skills, and motivating students); we also demonstrated the importance of improving teacher effectiveness in the classroom. Getting organized for instruction, the second crucial aspect of planning and organizing discussed in this chapter, focused on how peer consultants help teachers to improve their technical organization by streamlining everyday tasks and procedures. We discussed elements of lesson planning, the third crucial element of planning and organizing; in this section of the chapter we outlined numerous tips peer consultants shared with teachers to improve instruction. This chapter closed with a brief description of the dark side of planning and organizing; here, we provided descriptions of negative experiences from which teachers were able to derive positive learning. In Chapter 5 we discuss peer consultation skill #4, showing and sharing.

REMINDERS AND QUESTIONS

1. Planning is a time-consuming but critical element of teaching which can *make or break* a lesson. What are some different ways teachers in your school plan for instruction? Do any teachers plan collaboratively? If so, what advantages do they perceive in such work?

2. Disorganization in the classroom wastes valuable time and undermines student learning. How can teachers help each other to become better organized, limit unnecessary work, and achieve peer efficiency? How can administrators help in this endeavor?

3. Fellow teachers are the richest source of knowledge about essential planning elements and organizational tips. How can you expand opportunities for teachers to plan together and share tips?

SUGGESTED READING FOR FURTHER LEARNING

Maintaining High Expectations and
Developing Critical Thinking Skills

Caine, R. N., Caine, G., McClintic, C., & Klimek, K. (Eds.) (2005). *12 Brain/mind learning principles in action*. Alexandria, VA: Association for Supervision and Curriculum Development.

Jensen, E. (2005). *Teaching with the brain in mind.* Alexandria, VA: Association for Supervision and Curriculum Development.

Sousa, D. A. (2001). *How the special needs brain learns.* Alexandria, VA: Association for Supervision and Curriculum Development.

Sousa, D. A. (2003). *How the gifted brain learns.* Alexandria, VA: Association for Supervision and Curriculum Development.

Sylwester, R. (2005). *How to explain a brain: An educator's handbook of brain terms and cognitive processes.* Alexandria, VA: Association for Supervision and Curriculum Development.

Tomlinson, C. A., Kaplan, S. N., Renzulli, J., Purcell, J., Leppien, J., & Burns, D. (Eds.) (2002). *The parallel curriculum: A design to develop high potential and challenge high-ability learners.* Thousand Oaks, CA: Corwin Press.

Planning and Organizing for Teaching

Andrade, H. G. (2000). *Using rubrics to promote thinking and learning.* Alexandria, VA: Association for Supervision and Curriculum Development.

Burke, L. M. (2002). *The teacher's ultimate planning guide.* Thousand Oaks, CA: Corwin Press.

Hunter, R. (2004). *Madeline Hunter's mastery teaching: Increasing instructional effectiveness in elementary and secondary schools.* Thousand Oaks, CA: Corwin Press.

Jacobs, H. H. (2004). *Getting results with curriculum mapping.* Alexandria, VA: Association for Supervision and Curriculum Development.

Joyce, B., Weil, M., & Calhoun, E. (2000). *Models of teaching* (6th ed.). Needham Heights, MA: Allyn & Bacon.

Stergar, C. (2005). *Performance tasks, checklists, and rubrics.* Thousand Oaks, CA: Corwin Press.

Wachter, J. C., & Carhart, C. (Eds.) (2003). *Time-saving tips for teachers.* Thousand Oaks, CA: Corwin Press.

Walsh, J. A., & Sattes, B. D. (Eds.) (2005). *Quality questioning: Research-based practice to engage every learner.* Thousand Oaks, CA: Corwin Press.

Wilke, R. L. (2003). *The first days of class: A practice guide for the beginning teacher.* Thousand Oaks, CA: Corwin Press.

5

Peer Consultation Skill #4: Showing and Sharing

Teaching may be one of few professions in which practitioners generously and passionately help colleagues and do this in spite of numerous barriers. Because teaching is an intensely human endeavor, the nature of *showing* others (i.e., demonstrating how to perform important professional tasks) as well as *sharing* (i.e., giving others instructional materials and resources) takes on profound meaning for personal and professional growth, individual efficacy, and career success. In this chapter we describe multiple dimensions of peer consultation skill #4, showing and sharing, from the mundane and routine to the philosophical and esoteric. This includes the particular conceptual, content area, and strategy lessons that support classroom instruction, as well as the sharing of instructional materials and resources.

At the most basic level, for example, peer consultants helped teachers acclimate themselves to the school:

She called me when I began working at the school, took me to lunch, took me to the school, and gave me a tour.

I walked into an almost overwhelming situation with 23 first graders. She explained the setup for the year. She helped me throughout the year to understand logistical and administrative responsibilities as well as information about teaching. We laughed, cried, and played together while teaching children and we loved it.

Peer consultants also helped teachers prepare to teach:

She opened her classroom to me, gave me supplies, and answered all of my curriculum and developmental questions. She explained her techniques and even came into my class and explained it to the class. Then she asked me if she could model for me how to teach estimation.

She met with me weekly and we collaboratively planned lessons and brainstormed activities.

When I began teaching a new subject, he generously shared his plans for that subject with me and let me observe his teaching the subject. He mentored me through the process.

My peer gave me suggestions related to specific adaptations of my materials, learning opportunities, placement of items in the room, and supplementary materials.

More broadly, peer consultants revealed to their colleagues deep understandings of what it means to be a teacher and to teach well:

She was a student advocate; she stood up for what she believed even if it was unpopular.

My colleague teacher courageously stood up in a faculty meeting. Here the administrators were constantly distracting us from teaching; and she confronted the administrator in the meeting, saying that she felt it was ridiculous that teachers were being asked to do yet one more extra meeting. I realized that some faculty members were embarrassed by her rebellion, but I also know that teachers are not meant to be administration's puppets. Here we were put in that situation frequently and constantly by passing work down to us.

I learned an important lesson about diversity from him: that one-size curriculum does not fit all students.

What he said and stood for could fill many books; from him I learned the notion of "I do and I understand." It may not have been original, but he demonstrated how to never stop letting students "do."

In the remainder of this chapter, we specifically describe the kinds of lessons teachers learned from peer consultants' *showing*, learning by observing (another form of showing), and examples of sharing. Teachers' descriptions, taken directly from their experiences with collaborative work, best describe the significance and efficacy of peer consultation.

SHOWING: THREE KINDS OF LESSONS

Among the many forms of peer consultants' showing (or demonstrating), we identified three primary categories of lessons teachers learned, including conceptual lessons, content area lessons, strategy lessons, and a category of *other lessons* learned from peer consultants.

Conceptual Lessons

Through their classroom teaching and work-related actions, peer consultants demonstrated fundamental conceptual lessons about instruction to other teachers, including the importance of meaningful, active, and fun-filled instruction; the power of group work; the need to move from direct instruction to creative lessons; ways to support student learning through problem solving; and ways to incorporate exploration and experimentation in lessons. Figure 5.1 provides examples of conceptual lessons learned from peer consultants.

Content Area Lessons

Moreover, peer consultants had considerable experience and expertise in specific content areas; and they generously demonstrated the use of approaches, strategies, and materials for these content areas with teachers. Figure 5.2 provides numerous examples of ways that peer consultants showed effective content-specific teaching to their colleagues.

Strategy Lessons

We also found that peer consultants demonstrated *how to* use a wide variety of generic approaches and techniques in their teaching, regardless of content area and often across disciplines. For example, they might demonstrate how to hold debates (whether about political issues or physics theories), use journals, incorporate hands-on activities, do Web projects, or conduct a choral reading. Figure 5.3 presents examples of this form of showing.

Figure 5.1   Examples of Conceptual Lessons Teachers Learned From Peer
Consultants

She did a workshop that drove home the importance of exposing students to **meaningful reading and writing every day.** From him I learned a current events format that I use in class.

She taught me that children **learn by doing** and she showed me ways to keep them **actively engaged.**

He showed me how to adjust my **focus and pacing** tremendously in order to reach all my objectives during the year.

I watched her **make learning fun** for her students; they always come out of her classroom with knowledge that will help them with their school careers, with their careers as well. This also gave her the ability to **command respect** from the community as a person and a teacher. I hope that I am half the teacher that she is, and I admire her.

I watched a teacher in a brain-based school; none of the classes were traditional. Students were actively engaged in **groups and independent learning.**

He modeled the use of **concept maps.** I observed his students doing academic learning **group work** and transitions.

A classroom teacher taught me **direct instruction** and the parts of each lessons in direct instruction. This is particularly useful for first year teachers.

She taught a lesson on **problem solving.** I learned the problem doesn't have to be reading and computation only. I learned that using manipulatives and drawing pictures are important for some students.

She taught me how to use **metacognitive strategies** that help students rely on their own thinking and feelings. I then taught my students how self-talk can help them with their work and how to stay focused with their thinking.

He taught me how to do **exploration, conceptualization, and application**; the students brainstorm, they get the ideas formed, and they apply what they learned.

This teacher was a big help to me in terms of **creative instruction.** She showed me how to use a lot of projects and hands-on activities. She shared her ideas and enhanced my teaching as well as my student's excitement and learning.

He demonstrated how to use **conferencing** with the student as a way to improve instruction.

She compared the red marks a teacher makes on a child's paper to the red flag in front of a bull. It taught me how to **be careful of what I said** on each child's paper each and every day.

Other Lessons

Peer consultants also showed teachers ways to handle special education responsibilities, communicate with parents, take advantage of available resources, evaluate student progress, and manage students (classroom

Text continues on p. 89

Figure 5.2   Examples of Content Area Lessons Teachers Learned From Peer
Consultants

Reading

She described her **literacy circles, guided reading groups and self-selected parts of the reading program**; she showed me how to organize notebooks for each child and how they kept track of their work.

After I saw her **literacy centers** and that they were not disorganized and chaotic, I modeled my classroom after her approach.

He held a series of lessons on approaches to more **effective reading practices,** and he facilitated discussion of these practices.

He showed me how to make a **printout of vocabulary** and high frequency words for student readings; these are put in student's agenda books and learned prior to reading.

My peer teachers modeled **reading comprehension strategies** and a variety of topics related to the teaching of reading and writing.

She gave me the handout that she gives to parents who observe in her class and then modeled a reading recovery lesson. I learned how to prepare **math manipulatives in paper bags** prior to the lesson; this saves time and gets the children curious. They were more excited to learn.

She helped me develop a **unique way to involve students in literature.** We varied the ways in which students selected to report on their monthly novels; we experimented with it for several months and developed the ideas into literature circles. Students are excited; they read and share and they relate the characters to each other.

She demonstrated her technique for helping children write **bibliographies.**

She showed me how to do **interactive writing,** which helps with letter formations, spacing, sentence structure, etc.

She showed me how to teach **spelling** in a special way by "making words." It makes much more sense and teaches the students why things are spelled certain ways. It is a very effective way of teaching spelling compared to the traditional spelling tests where words are just memorized and soon forgotten.

She showed me how to use **letter cards** to help students improve their vocabulary; it was fun and effective and I adopted the strategy.

She taught me to use the **reader's theater** in my language arts and social studies class.

She shared examples and **strategies for guiding reading lessons**.

Math

A fellow teacher at our grade level gave an in-service lesson and showed us **activities** that we could use **to teach various math skills**.

He demonstrated the **step-by-step process of teaching graphs,** including titles, researching figures, and constructing the graph using a web site. There was great attention to detail and method, which is often overlooked in teaching graphs.

I was out of my element when I first started teaching. I was having a hard time because I remembered math as just being about flash cards—at least in my own experience—and it certainly didn't work my students. Fortunately, he showed me how to use a **variety of manipulatives.**

She modeled a great **math activity** at the beginning of every month; I was able to observe this.

(Continued)

Figure 5.2 (Continued)

She showed me how to use **M&Ms** to teach bar graphs.

He introduced me to the Web site for **stock market games.**

She taught me a little **competition for the times tables**; students go around the room standing beside others whom they challenge. The objective is to be the first to respond and then to move all the way around the room. This teacher gives every student a card with a number or a term on it as they enter the room; it sparks their interest.

They have **different aged kids sit in different places in the car when they go for a ride** according to whether we are working on addition or subtraction.

This teacher shared with me how she organizes her **math center rotations**—centers that help enrich students that need basic skills— modeled guided reading groups, demonstrated interactive writing, showed me a method of using math centers in the classroom.

Social Studies

He showed me how to **re-engineer the entire social studies program** into four themes in which major events are post-holed and others serve as wire connecting them.

He showed me many methods of teaching and many hands-on approaches to social studies concepts such as **drawing human globes with chalk,** putting in an equator, north and south poles, the hemispheres, etc.

She showed me how to organize **social studies lessons by themes** rather than by chronological order; for example, how economics affect history, the impact of immigration, civil rights and civil wrongs, and the U.S. as a world power.

She went to a class that I couldn't attend and then came back and taught us the **new social studies curriculum**; took time after class to go over the new material with me and helped me be better prepared to teach.

This teacher showed me how to use **regalia in teaching** world geography; he had flags, taught us a German drinking song, and shared his experiences overseas.

He showed me how to use **role-playing** in political science.

Science

I watched him answer a difficult **question about radiation** that I, myself, could not answer. It helped me link more concepts together in my own mind.

She showed me about successful **methods for teaching horticulture,** gave me examples of successful hands-on lessons she had used.

She turned her entire classroom into a **functioning ecosystem.** The students devoted a portion of each day to creating or maintaining the various environments.

Foreign Languages and Music

A teacher friend showed me how to use **songs**—like *Twinkle, Twinkle Little Star*—to help students learn Latin declensions.

He gave me the idea of using a **game called Around the World**; it is a vocabulary game for use in Spanish classes.

This teacher showed me how to use **popular music** examples to teach fundamental music techniques; for example, in teaching form the teacher played pop music and had the students listen to key changes, then using more formal classical styles of music, she had the students compare and contrast.

Figure 5.3   Examples of Strategy Lessons Teachers Learned From Peer
Consultants

After twenty-eight years of teaching, I learned about the **brain gym** from him. It has had a profound effect on my students. It is about twenty-six movements that activate both sides of the brain so the whole brain can be involved in learning; it organizes students, gets them focused, and helps them to communicate; it also changes their behavior because of their being focused.

An English teacher showed me how to prepare students to give speeches in classes to form **debates** and how to reward winners.

He demonstrated a **mock jury trial.** Students have to **research** their roles and the topic and they become very involved.

He showed me how to organize my ideas and hands-on approach to learning for a variety of subjects; the students learned **mime, monologues, dialogue, and portraiture.**

He showed me a game called Get One, Give One in which students move around the room **getting facts** that they didn't previously have from other students and in turn giving each student a fact.

He showed me how to have students use a **journal** to review their assigned readings and reactions to the readings.

He showed me how to use **novels** to teach reading comprehension.

He showed me how to use **role-playing,** acting out skills the students were learning.

She demonstrated how to make up **stories** about characters they already know to help them learn. I might start with "papa bear, mama bear, and bear are a family. . . ."

He taught me how to make **theme books** and then form lessons around them.

She showed me how to help students **create a paper, try it out in some way in the classroom, and then reflect on it** as part of doing the paper.

This teacher demonstrated how to motivate students using **hands-on** activities.

I learned how to use an **exercise or a dance routine** to help students learn prepositions.

I learned how to have students **vote on issues** by placing themselves on a continuum in the room; it might be a vote about a class rule, a character in a novel, or a theme in a lesson, for example.

One teacher taught me how to use a blank **transparency** on top of my diagrams so that I can write on them without destroying them.

She demonstrated how to draw a big hand on the board and have students trace their own hands in their notebooks and how to use this for **webbing,** with the main idea in the palm and supporting details in the fingers. It is simple and effective.

She had students do a **research project** based on the day they born, and then she **graded the process** instead of the product.

She incorporated lots of projects into her inclusion classes so students could apply their learning to their daily lives; for example, for physical science they researched an element and then brought in **examples of items in which that element could be found.**

(Continued)

Figure 5.3 (Continued)

She taught me a completely different approach to teaching. It worked so well that I have used it and developed it to meet my students' needs. I learned to use strategies like **webbing** to help students integrate new material or review older material.

She taught me how to use **choral reading** in class and to involve students and the teacher in choral reading, paragraph by paragraph.

She taught me to give students hands-on experiences whenever possible. For example; we do a **parenting quilt** for the women's shelter, we do a **make-a-birdhouse for fractions** and **ecosystem-in-a-jar** for biology, build **lamps** for physical science, operated a **school store** and made **paper** for thank you notes for English class.

Figure 5.4   Examples of Other Lessons Teachers Learned From Peer Consultants (Special Education, Parent Contact, Evaluation, Use of Resources, and Student Management)

Special Education

She explained differences in procedures for **using IQ scores**—important differences because they were used differently in my previous experience.

She had a great **organizational tool** for all the students going through the special education evaluation procedures. Her file drawer was divided into sections such as ready to test, need to observe, waiting on vision and hearing, ready for parent conference, etc.

She showed me how to **write IEPs** [individual educational plans] or individual student program goals.

He helped me see how **people tend to be negative towards things about which they are ignorant and see how to deal with it.** For example, I have to walk to two or three classes every thirty minutes (because children are embarrassed to walk themselves to speech therapy at middle school age so I have to go and get them); he explained that teachers might think that I don't do anything but walk around. This helped me realize that people scorn the unknown and I know need to keep my colleagues better informed.

Parent Contact

It was my first year in a large metro school district; I was teaching second grade in a portable classroom and parent night was looming on the horizon. I was in a panic as to how to present the curriculum and other things to my parents. My neighbor teacher came to the rescue. She took time out of her hectic schedule to walk me through all of these matters step by step. She taught me **how to keep attendance and behavioral information in my grade book** so that when parents came for conferences, I would be able to explain exactly how the students were doing.

She showed me how she devotes a **planning period** every week to making telephone calls to parents.

She wrote me an **encouraging note** when I was going through a difficult time with a parent, something I appreciated so much that I will someday do the same for other teachers.

She showed me how she relates to a student by relating to her parents: by **developing a relationship** with them because they are the most important individuals in the child's life.

I saw how this teacher **sent home a poem** every evening for a week so parents could help their children every night while the children read the poems to their parents.

Figure 5.4 (Continued)

Evaluation

She showed me the strategy of **presenting criteria for assignments graphically,** not verbally.

She taught me how to do **collaborative team analyses** of students' progress.

Using Resources

He showed me how to use a variety of classroom resources; for example, I had no idea that you could **mark on pull down maps.** It is great to help students visualize.

This teacher encouraged me to use all of my resources, including **audio and visual aids** to assist in student learning.

I needed materials desperately, so **he guided me** through the grant-writing project.

He asked us to keep a box **for a week into which we placed all ditto sheets** that we asked children to complete. This emphasized the importance of varying our lessons; not using merely one type of activity, the same old thing.

Managing Students

She showed me how to use **specific and different ways of communicating** with students.

Her sixth grade room that I observed ran itself. I was impressed; she helped me with **management strategies** and gave me some tips.

She explained her **discipline system,** which involved a variety of extrinsic and intrinsic rewards as well as positive and negative consequences.

---

management will be discussed in detail in Chapter 6). Figure 5.4 includes examples of this type of showing. By comparing teachers' reports about conceptual, content, strategy, and other lessons learned from peer consultants with recent summaries of research-driven practices that enhance student progress across content areas (Figure 5.5), we concluded that peer consultants' assistance is clearly congruent with effective practice. Thus it is a powerful way for teachers to approach instructional improvement. We recommend that all peer consultants compare their learning with the practices described in Cawelti's (2004) empirical research across content areas.

THE POWER OF LEARNING BY OBSERVING: A SPECIAL FORM OF SHOWING

Clearly, from our findings about showing presented thus far, teachers learned to teach by observing peer consultants and by being observed by them. Indeed, both afforded teachers an opportunity to reflect on and improve instruction. Observing peer consultants gave teachers a chance to

Figure 5.5   Enhancing Student Progress Through Research-Driven Practices Across Content Areas

Effective General Practices

Parental involvement

Graded homework

Aligned time on task

Direct teaching

Advance organizers

Teaching of learning strategies tutoring

Mastery learning

Cooperative learning

Adaptive education

Effective Practices in the Content Areas

The Arts

Direct instruction

Immediate feedback

Interdisciplinary learning

Questioning techniques

Reflecting on learning and nonlearning

Individual performance

Use of creative drama and theater

Visual and aural thinking

Sequencing for understanding

Use of psychomotor principles

Correct body use

Improving memory

Instruction in the role of symbols

Nonverbal aids to reading

Focus on the arts as separate disciplines

Arts and special needs students

Understanding of culture in and through the arts

Foreign Language

Begin instruction early

Language acquisition and opportunities for interaction

Communicative language practice

Instruction in learning strategies

Instruction in listening and reading for meaning

Writing instruction

Explicit grammar instruction

Integration of culture

Appropriate assessment of student progress

Use of technology

Health Education

Developing personal competence

Developing social competence

Practice in goal setting and decision making

Development of values awareness

Practice in critical analysis of health information

Activity-oriented, interactive learning

Using the student as teacher

Encouraging and developing parental involvement

Language Arts

Extensive reading

Interactive learning

Extension of background knowledge

Instruction in strategic reading and writing

Interrelated activities

Teaching critical reading and writing skills

Discussion and analysis

Emphasis on the writing process

Balanced reading and writing

Early intervention

Exposure to a range of literature

Appropriate assessment

Oral Communication

Improving oral communication competence

Addressing voice and articulation

Reducing oral communication anxiety

Emphasizing communication ethics

Facilitating interpersonal and small group communication

Increasing listening effectiveness

Developing media literacy

Figure 5.5 (Continued)

Mathematics	Wait time
Opportunity to learn	Concept mapping
Focus on learning	Computer simulations
Learning new concepts and skills while solving problems	Microcomputer-based laboratories
Opportunities for invention and practice	Systematic approaches in problem solving
Openness to student solution methods and student interaction	Conceptual understanding in problem solving
Small group learning	Science technology society
Whole class discussion	Real life situations
Number sense	Discrepant events
Concrete materials	
Student use of calculators	**Social Studies**
	Thoughtful classrooms
Physical Education	Jurisprudential teaching
	Appropriate classroom environment
Time for practice	Teaching critical thinking
Appropriate, meaningful practice	Support for concept development
Cognitive engagement	Effective questioning
Content sequencing	Cognitive prejudice reduction
Spiral curriculum	Computer technology
Developmental program focus	Student participation in the community
Administrative support	Constructivist teaching
Science	
Learning cycle approach	
Collaborative learning	
Analogies	

NOTE: For more information, see Cawelti (2004).

see good teaching in action and to learn how to handle specific content and strategies in the context of live classrooms:

> The resource teacher let me observe her teaching using our adopted reading method. I saw how she set it up, how she organized her materials, what she did with other students, etc. She gave me all the activities and labs that she does and explained any concepts with which I wasn't comfortable.

> I saw a videotape of this teacher; it was quality teaching in a very successful school.

> I observed her implementing literacy centers.

I saw a teacher model interactive writing in a large group situation.

I watched her do an interactive writing assignment with the students.

She let me watch how she taught literature circles, having a discussion director, vocabulary "enricher," summarizer artist, literary luminary, etc.

I observed a teacher whose teaching expanded my repertoire of therapeutic techniques for exceptional students.

She demonstrated the use of picture books to teach each part separately. It was loaded with figurative language to help students understand why authors present ideas in different ways.

She held a mock trial of Beowulf, who had been accused of murdering a dragon, and invited me to be a witness for the defense team.

She modeled both a visual and auditory means of giving instructions so she could reach more diverse groups of learners.

To be sure, modeling by peer consultants had a powerful influence on teachers; in fact, they often emulated what they observed in their own classroom instruction:

Now my students make myth bags. It is simply a lunch bag decorated to reflect the myth with three things about the myth on it. For example, for the myth of Orpheus and Eurydice, each student decorated the bag with a snake and a musical instrument, the lyre.

I learned how to use maps, journals, tourist brochures, and team competitions to help students learn world studies; the students gain ownership and allegiance to their groups and the peer pressure forces them to do as well as they can.

After observing her and adapting her technique to my class, I now know that making someone the center of attention can have an extremely positive effect on them as a learner.

As mentioned earlier, being observed by peer consultants provided additional opportunities to learn about good teaching:

During my first year of teaching another teacher had a profound impact on my teaching. She was taking a course and one of her requirements was to observe and confer with another teacher. She did this with me. At first she just watched, then we talked about my goals and methods. We worked on planning, how to begin class, and she gave suggestions on motivation. She observed me again and coached me through it. After we stopped, I continued using her suggestions and my students even commended me on how I had improved. She provided books I could research on my own and helped me structure my class period with warm-ups and cool-downs.

She did an observation of my teaching for a class that she was taking. I learned so much from this experience and it made me think about my own teaching, my style, my strengths and weaknesses.

He observed my teaching and then afterward we discussed it; this encouraged my reflection, as I was able to picture my class through his eyes. He even took time later to go over writing samples with me so I would feel more confident in staging and grading papers.

After observing me, he used me as a model for other teachers; I demonstrated the correct way to perform a specific skill, which boosted my self-esteem.

This teacher observed my classroom and offered some ideas about modifications that would improve my teaching; it made me think more carefully about my teaching.

SHARING: A BOUNTY FROM COLLEAGUES

Not only did peer consultants show or demonstrate how to teach, they frequently and liberally *shared* a wealth of instructional materials and resources with teachers. The following data illustrate peer consultants' generous giving to teachers, giving that largely determined teachers' effectiveness:

She opened her files, let me go through them, and told me to take whatever I wanted and make copies of it.

He loaned me a book on your first year as an elementary school teacher.

A teacher shared comprehension questions that she had compiled to accompany grade level reading work.

One of the teachers made a master list and a file of all available resources within the school for each program. Resources can be utilized within the different programs in the same building and duplication is reduced.

He organized and shared a series of math exemplars for the whole grade level. He shared resources, materials, and ideas that I could use and incorporate into my curriculum.

She gave me additional resources for enriching my classroom, experiments, hands-on activities, books, and materials that could actually be used in different activities with microscopes, slides, and chemicals.

She gave me a Web site address that contains special and specific information about a curriculum for special education students learning functional skills.

SUMMARY

This chapter highlighted peer consultation skill #4, showing and sharing. We began by describing how peer consultants helped teachers acclimate themselves to the school, provided teachers with information about the culture of teaching, and generally helped teachers understand what it means to be a good teacher. The centerpiece of the chapter included detailed descriptions of *showing and sharing,* that is, how peer consultants demonstrated valuable conceptual lessons, content area lessons, and strategy lessons to teachers; how they generously opened their classrooms for mutual peer observation; and how they shared critical resources and materials with teachers to improve teaching effectiveness. Chapter 6 describes peer consultation skill #5, guiding for classroom management.

IMPLICATIONS FOR PRACTICE AND QUESTIONS

1. All teachers need to open their classroom doors to colleagues to build a culture of openness and trust. As teachers become more comfortable visiting each other's classrooms, they will naturally share their observations and reflections with each other, making your school a frequent topic among teachers, because it is a place where experimentation and risk taking are welcome. What steps are necessary to create or enhance a culture of showing and sharing in your school?

2. Administrators should liberally promote the healthy culture that can spring up among educators, one of generous showing and

sharing; this eases and invigorates the routine, but highly complex, work of helping students learn. What steps can administrators take to enhance and extend *showing and sharing* among teachers?

3. Specifically, rather than assuming that teachers can do this important work on the fly and without support, how can administrators provide needed time and resources—as well as symbolic support—to teachers who want to collaborate?

SUGGESTED READING FOR FURTHER LEARNING

Observing and Teacher Talk

Achinstein, B. (Ed.) (2005). *Mentors in the making: Developing new leaders for new teachers.* New York: Teachers College Press.

Allen, D. W. & LeBlanc, A. C. (2004*). Collaborative peer coaching that improved instruction.* Thousand Oaks, CA: Corwin Press.

Clark, M. C. (2001). *Talking shop: Authentic conversation and teacher learning.* Alexandria, VA: Association for Supervision and Curriculum Development.

Johnson, T. (2002). *Improving instruction through observation and feedback.* Alexandria, VA: Association for Supervision and Curriculum Development.

Knowles, M. S., Holton, E. F., & Swanson, R. A. (1998). *The adult learner: The definitive classic in adult education and human resources development.* Alexandria, VA: Association for Supervision and Curriculum Development.

McGuire, V. J., & Duff, C. (2004). *Conversations about being a teacher.* Thousand Oaks, CA: Corwin Press.

Mezirow, J. (2000). *Learning to think like an adult.* Alexandria, VA: Association for Supervision and Curriculum Development.

Nieto, S. (Ed.) (2005). *Why we teach.* New York: Teachers College Press.

Sherin, M. (2000). *Viewing teaching on videotape.* Alexandria, VA: Association for Supervision and Curriculum Development.

Tileston, D. W. (2005). *Ten best teaching practices: How brain research, learning styles, and standards define teaching competencies.* Thousand Oaks, CA: Corwin Press.

Action Research

Calhoun, E. M. (1994). *How to use action research in the self-renewing school.* Alexandria, VA: Association for Supervision and Curriculum Development.

Langer, G. M., Colton, A. B., & Goff, L. S. (2003). *Collaborative analysis of student work: Improving teaching and learning.* Alexandria, VA: Association for Supervision and Curriculum Development.

Poetter, T., McKamey, C., Ritter, C., & Tisdel, P. (1999). *Emerging profiles of teacher-mentors as researchers: Benefits of shared inquiry.* Alexandria, VA: Association for Supervision and Curriculum Development.

Sagor, R. (2000). *Guiding school improvement with action research.* Alexandria, VA: Association for Supervision and Curriculum Development.

Sagor, R. (2005). *The action research guidebook: A four-step process for educators and school teams.* Thousand Oaks, CA: Corwin Press.

6

Peer Consultation Skill #5: Guiding for Classroom Management

This chapter begins with descriptions of the downside of classroom management: *horror stories* in which teachers witnessed students humiliated, demeaned, and threatened by other teachers. This is followed by a presentation of findings from our study on the numerous ways that peer consultants help teachers effect positive classroom management as it relates to academics and student needs, the *love* approach, student responsibility, a calm demeanor, depersonalizing, consistency, misguided goals, proactivity, and restraint.

Many teachers' horrific experiences occurred in the distant past (when teachers were interning, for example), but others were more recent; nevertheless, all made strong impressions on teachers, and all served to strengthen their resolve to implement constructive approaches to classroom management:

> Every person's journey to knowledge is important and should be measured by the growth one experiences. I saw a teacher use criticism, unfounded anger, and public humiliation when students asked questions. It showed me how not to treat students, and hopefully, it will pop into my conscience and thinking the next time I struggle with a student.

This teacher would threaten students who were misbehaving but never follow through; it led to a disorganized environment where students thought it was okay to misbehave. I thought if procedures, rules, and consequences were put in place they should be adhered to. I realized that I should mean what I say and say what I mean in the classroom.

His class was boring, and he was very negative in his approach to the children. I didn't want to turn out like him, doing the same thing over and over and being negative. Every year I look for something new, positive, and different to go with each unit I teach.

Witnessing other teachers yelling at students was particularly distressing:

I observed a teacher who yelled constantly throughout the day at her students. It reinforced my belief in not raising your voice unless absolutely necessary. Her actions were degrading to students and the students tuned her out eventually. Now I strive to use various other strategies to control classroom environment. I rarely raise my voice and I never speak in a degrading manner to students.

I watched a teacher yell at her students in the hallway during my first year of teaching; the scene really struck a chord with me, such that I vowed to never allow myself to reach the point where I raised my voice at a student. This brought into focus more closely the importance of being consistent and firm enough so as to avoid escalating situations.

My next door teacher colleague is a woman who yells at her students, is very sarcastic, and constantly uses put-downs. Some of my children attend her math class and they return with comments like, "She scares me," or "I am frightened there." At first, I was angry; how do people like this continue to get contracts? I was frustrated. Now, I protect my children who attend her class. They ask me questions instead of directing them to her. I will not yell or be sarcastic; my children are my babies.

NINE GUIDING PRINCIPLES OF CLASSROOM MANAGEMENT

Although teachers became highly motivated and were able to learn important lessons about proper classroom management from negative modeling, it was often work with peer consultants that made the critical difference in learning effective approaches to classroom management. They helped teachers by offering *tips* about classroom routines (which we discussed in Chapter 5) and generally by modeling and reflective talk, what we call the Nine Guiding Principles of Classroom Management. Our data indicate that peer consultants, drawing from their experience and expertise, ascribed to and shared the following principles.

Principle #1: Match Academics to Student Needs

From peer consultants, teachers learned the importance of matching academics to students' needs; students whose needs are not being met are more likely to misbehave, perhaps because of boredom or frustration:

> When I was experiencing the typical management and discipline problems exhibited by most first year teachers, my colleague advised me to "take them from where they are." She realized that I was teaching over the heads of my students and that I was ignoring many behavioral and procedural concerns in favor of academic ones. The advice was the most meaningful advice I have received to date; it is prominent in my mind whenever I perform any planning or teaching task. The effect of the teacher's advice was to cause me to focus more on my students' needs, and it encouraged me to think about goals and directions for my students. Where do I want them to be by the end of the year and how will they get there? I began sequencing materials in smaller chunks, explaining concepts more clearly and choosing the lessons and learning experiences more carefully so most—if not all—students could feel successful.

Principle #2: Take a *Love* (Constructive) Approach

Peer consultants taught teachers that children needed warmth and encouragement and to use a *love* approach (i.e., caring, constructive, supportive); at the same time, they cautioned teachers about the difficulties of maintaining such an approach within busy classrooms:

> I noticed that she had a wonderful rapport with students, a positive atmosphere and a feeling of cooperation in the class. I asked her about it and she shared her management plan with me. She had a system of compliments for students, all positive; it changed my approach to classroom management for the better. Now I approach classroom management in a positive way. Students earn compliments and receiving them changes the atmosphere of the classroom; there is a much more encouraging atmosphere for learning.

> In an inservice session, he taught me about "love and logic." It has had a large effect on my teaching and the way I run a classroom. I think through the logical outcomes and results of children's actions and thoughts. My teaching has changed in that it is much more calm

and professional. When there are interruptions I assist children in thinking and making better decisions.

One teacher explained that she learned about the appropriate limits to relationships with students from her peer consultant:

I learned to be a friend, not a pal to my students. There is a difference, and I realized there must be good classroom management in order for learning to take place. It's not about wanting students to like me.

Principle #3: Insist on Student Responsibility and Invoke Natural Consequences

Teachers learned a valuable lesson. Students must be taught to assume responsibility for their conduct. When they make mistakes, they must face natural and appropriate consequences:

I learned that students should take responsibility for their actions; students choose to follow or not to follow rules. I believe behaviors can be controlled, and it is my job to teach students to take responsibility for their actions.

When this teacher was talking with a student, she emphasized her own positive expectations for the student and how the student had let her down. She made it so personal that the child responded; she did not want to let the teacher down. This same child had been a real challenge in other teachers' classes. I saw firsthand the importance of building a relationship, a true relationship with your students [based on] mutual respect, concern, and obligation. Until then I had not really believed that fostering a relationship with my students was so important. I was reluctant to demand a certain level of performance or behavior from them.

I learned that when a child behaves inappropriately you should invoke the natural consequences and then move on. I don't need to argue my point. We both know what is expected. I give the direction, wait for compliance, and give consequences if compliance doesn't follow.

Principle #4: Remain Calm and Composed

Peer consultants taught teachers that maintaining a relatively calm and composed demeanor—even when disciplining students—was critical for effective classroom management:

I watched a kindergarten teacher quietly handle discipline with dignity. She never raised her voice or humiliated or embarrassed any children. I try to do the same with children.

A very wise teacher taught me that the less you say, the less you have to regret later. She suggested nonverbal signs or walking around the room works better and she is right. Sometimes new teachers run into students who are determined to have the last word; logic has no effect on them and any comment from the teacher brings another answer. This can go on forever until the teacher gets mad, and nothing is accomplished except wasting class time and alienating the student. I have seen the disasters that result from arguing about insignificant things with teenagers. Now I try to find another way to get my students' attention. I can accomplish my goal of getting a student back on task without wasting everyone's time.

I saw him discipline a group and he appeared to be moderately but appropriately angry. At the same time, he remained completely calm and in control; most of the students even returned to apologize. This helps me not to become truly angry. My students respect me and they are more receptive.

I observed another teacher handle especially difficult children. Now I do what she did: I clearly think through my reactions and what the reactions of my behaviors from the students might be. I always remain calm and respond to students in relaxed manner. I don't put the student on the defensive and I don't argue.

I never had a course or any preparation for classroom management. I learned all my behavior management from watching other teachers. It helped me to see things that worked. I used the "clap your hands once if you hear my voice" technique to quiet a large group. It is better than yelling! Blinking the lights also works.

He taught me the power of quiet discipline. He worked to modify, not to punish inappropriate behavior. I learned that many students will act out in order to be removed from an uncomfortable situation and that I should not let them have their way. I should keep them in class and continue teaching them. Maintaining control is the teacher's responsibility. All children need to be in class as much as possible, not in the office or the suspension room or the time-out classroom.

Principle #5: Don't Take It Personally

What teachers learned from peer consultants abounds in the simple principle: Do not take things personally, a principle closely related to being calm and quiet in matters of discipline:

> He taught me not to take things personally and not to raise my voice unless totally necessary. It helped me gain and maintain control of my class, allowed me to teach, and allowed my students to learn. Now, I have more control when I keep my composure. I have decreased hindrances to my teaching and increased my ability to teach.

> She said not to take a child's misbehavior or lack of respect personally, and my reaction is now separated from what students do. It has affected classroom behavior; the students know I am not going to lose my cool and I have fewer disruptions.

Principle #6: Be Consistent

Consistency was another essential principle teachers learned from peer consultants. One teacher described this lesson as, "Say what you mean, and mean what you say":

> Say what you mean and mean what you say, that's what I learned from him! I stop and think before I say certain things. I know I must be able to back up my words with action, so I am accurate with what I say.

> I learned to "do what you say you are going to do." Whether it is an academic matter or behavior matter, you should always follow through or the students will not respect what you say. Now I don't say things unless I intend them. The students see me as stricter, but also consistent.

Fairness was frequently discussed as a corollary of consistency:

> Her classroom management was excellent and she was always fair and consistent with her students. It made me examine my management techniques and try to be fair with all students.

Principle #7: Consider Students' Misguided Goals When Misbehaving

Teachers in our study learned valuable lessons from peer consultants about student misbehavior and students' misguided goals:

She taught me about the goals of student misbehavior: attention seeking, defiance, revenge, and apathy or giving up. She showed me how to handle them. Now I think about the payoff and the goals for bad behavior, and I address it successfully. I have more time for teaching when the atmosphere in the room is positive and the students feel they are part of the team; something that is good.

I kept finding myself in power struggles with a student who seemed to hold all power. I shared my frustration with this teacher and she suggested ways to get him to be my helper and ways to win him over by giving him attention that he tried get in negative ways. I have used her suggestions ever since.

Principle #8: Be Proactive

Teachers in our study reported that being proactive was another critical classroom management principle they learned from peer consultants:

I learned to be proactive instead of reactive, to prevent problems that would become bigger later, to take care of things on the front end instead of at the back end. I realized that with so many different personalities and so much social interaction in the class, there are bound to be differences. Now I move around the room constantly, pick their brains, and read their minds to prevent problems.

I learned that when the students reverted to play time, I had to control them through the tone of my voice, separating students in different parts of the room, and removing the toys. I became a more structured teacher. I realized that I had to nip problems in the bud before they got out of control, so I became more assertive with students.

Principle # 9: Don't Overdo It

Peer consultants, according to our data, advised teachers to avoid overdoing classroom management (i.e., overreacting to and overtreating small issues) and to emphasize learning and student engagement:

I had been feeling as if I should address every incident of misconduct from serious to miniscule. I quickly became overwhelmed. My fellow teacher told me to "choose my battles," so I began separating what was truly disruptive from the rest, and I dealt with those incidents. This relieved me of a lot of stress and allowed me to concentrate on teaching. I began to think more like a teacher and less like a policeman. I realized that before I had changed, teaching was becoming secondary and keeping order was taking a priority.

My teaching naturally improved and there were fewer and smaller discipline issues occurring. I attribute this to the students becoming more engaged.

SETTING UP AND MAINTAINING CLASSROOM ROUTINES

Operationally speaking, peer consultants taught teachers how to set up and maintain classroom routines, from seating arrangements to working with diverse populations. Much of the advice given by peer consultants was in the form of *tips* or modeling; examples are presented in Figure 6.1.

Figure 6.1   Lessons From Peer Consultants About Setting Up and Maintaining Classroom Routines

---

Begin the Year Right

A teacher's main concern for the first week of school is not necessarily academics but developing classroom procedures. **Procedures, procedures, procedures.**

He taught me a valuable lesson: for the first and second week of school you shouldn't spend an enormous amount of time on instruction. **Your focus should be classroom management**: teaching them how to enter the classroom, if necessary; lining them up in the hall; having an activity when they enter; keeping rules to a minimum; reteaching and reinforcing appropriate behavior; and not losing your cool. I realized that my undergraduate preparation included no preparation for classroom management, and that I suffered and paid dearly because of that.

The way you want your students to behave at the end of the year is related to the way you start the beginning of the year. **I revisit my procedures** any time I need to.

She told me that you need to **start off tight and then let up** because if you start off loose then you never regain control. She explained her **discipline procedures** and then modeled them in her teaching. I keep this philosophy in mind: to be tough, tough at first.

"Don't smile until after the Christmas holidays." I was told by a veteran teacher that students can take kindness as a weakness and that regardless of how motivating my lesson was, and that if I didn't **focus on student discipline,** I would be an ineffective teacher.

"Don't smile for the first month." Set structure and the rules at the beginning of the year; let students know the expectations from the start. I had wanted the students to like me and enjoy school, and I was concerned this strategy would be in conflict with that; but I realized that learning takes place when there is order and structure.

I heard that Harry Wong said, **"You will either win or lose your class on the first day of school."** It is true. My way of thinking has changed dramatically. Instead of surviving the first days of school, I now use them to lay the groundwork and foundation for the rest of the year. Now I use **procedures** in every area of my day and activities because they are critical to the functioning of the classroom. Students know what is expected and things run more smoothly, and I am able to cover much more material.

I learned **what the rules should be, how to post them, and how to enforce them.** It cuts down on time to get the class settled, and I have more time to teach and for questions.

Figure 6.1 (Continued)

She told me to **start with a rule about students staying in their seats.** I had been allowing too much free roaming by students. I thought this was too restrictive, but it helped my discipline. It also helped my teaching in general because I didn't have to worry about unnecessary interruptions.

Have Plans and Systems

He gave me a copy of his **classroom management plan** from which I was able to create my own plan; I understood the value of having a consistent daily routine and a structured predictable environment. I think about and understand the needs of my students; students are ready to learn, and I am a more successful teacher.

She had a **system for everything,** questions on the board for when students entered the same routine all year long. The students knew what to expect. I began to focus on my management techniques, and it improved my ability to teach because I could focus on teaching, not management.

Overplan so students are always engaged. I had wondered, can't students sit quietly for a while? But discipline problems are more likely to occur when students are not involved.

I was a floating middle school teacher and she taught me **organizational skills** that work for floaters; I learned that even though I am not in my own room, I can still teach a lot of material. Today, clear expectations are my first priority.

Use Warm-ups

Use **warm-ups at the beginning of class** to help settle the class down. For example; I use correcting sentences as warm-ups. This makes an easy transition into the day's lesson.

Use Signals

The teacher **raised his hand** as students entered the classroom and immediately the class became quiet. The teacher then got the students immediately engaged instead of wasting time by verbally taking roll; instead it was done silently.

He got his students in line by saying, **"quiet as a mouse, still as a rock, one, two, three."** He didn't raise his voice. Students respond well to quiet directions and more time can be spent on teaching.

Use Proximity

The teacher **moved around the room** almost continuously as he was teaching. The students were quiet and remained on task. This helped keep discipline problems down.

I try to reach all my students at all levels. I continually **circle the room** and check for their understanding.

Adjust Seating

The students were all in rows in my classes ("ticky tacky, all in pretty little boxes and rows"). He gave me a suggestion to face them away from the door, so they wouldn't be distracted by folks going past in the hall. This conversation helped me think about other ways to help students interact. I tried **numerous arrangements** over the years with varying degrees of success depending on the age level and size of the class.

She removed all the desks from her room and **arranged it by tables in a U design**. I realized there is not just one way to arrange a classroom and that environment is very important for the students and their needs. This gave me more physical control of my class. I could better see who needed help and monitor behaviors.

(Continued)

Figure 6.1 (Continued)

Track Misbehaviors

Find a way to **keep track of and record** students' behaviors and other information about the students. I also use incentives, which work with technical level as well as college prep students. I have fewer behavior problems.

In a class in which we had many behaviorally disabled students, he showed me how to **make a board, a visual display, reflecting problem behaviors.** On the board, we tallied behaviors and students could see visually what they had done. Within two weeks we no longer needed the board. I realize that many different strategies are valuable and you choose depending on what works best with the particular group of students. This helped them to remember rules. We maintained structure and order in the classroom and made class more enjoyable for everyone.

Experiment With Varied Techniques According to the Students' Issues

She demonstrated the **"1–2–3 magic" technique** with a student who had behavior problems. It's an effective way to discipline in which the child always knows the consequences, and it causes less disruption when disciplining a child.

This teacher had an excellent relationship with the students whom I had found difficult to manage. She showed me some of the techniques she used that worked with him. This made me think about my relationship with the student and why I was reacting to his behavior in such a manner. It gave me a chance to reflect. Then I used **different techniques** to create a better relationship with him.

As a support teacher I learned that **constant interaction** between me and the lead teacher is useful for avoiding problems and confrontations with students. We began interacting frequently; this also provided a good model for the students: appropriate adult interactions. Now I realize there are many strategies one could use in working with these special students; I came to know which strategy to use when.

She used the **"silent" plan,** allowing no talking whatsoever for a certain period of time. Students were given individual seatwork. It was her way of getting behavior in a class under control. It made me aware that there are many ways a teacher can manipulate the environment to get a desired result. I transferred this idea to another situation where students could not handle close proximity.

He taught me a **group contingency plan,** whereby a misbehaving child affects group privileges. Initially, I wasn't sure it was ethical, then I found out it works, and it reduced disruptions.

She taught me to **not put the equipment out for kindergarten students while I am giving directions,** because they tend to play with it, instead of listening. Now the students follow instructions well.

He has students **lend him something** (like, for example, their shoes) if they use his materials. If they don't get them back until they return the materials, they never forget. I think it is good to add a little humor; it is a fair trade, and it removed the hassle of writing lists of names or losing materials.

When I worked in a rural, very poor school district, a teacher showed me how to do a **Friday afternoon cooking and tasting experience** for students who had demonstrated good behaviors during the week. The next day a veteran teacher commented on all the neat things I had done in my class. I was surprised that she even noticed. This encouraged me. I realized maybe I was on the right track with these students.

Figure 6.1 (Continued)

Working with extremely difficult students, I never realized the **importance of humor** in de-escalating potentially explosive situations. The teacher used the strategy frequently and I saw its positive effects in avoiding crises. It also helped to develop a good everyday social skill for the students and they modeled it in the interactions with others. I realized I was too serious and that humor could help as a management strategy; something I had never considered before. This gave me a wonderful tool to use.

Use Body Language

I watched him teach and saw how he successfully handled the class clown's misbehavior. It opened my eyes to things like **body language and subconscious behavior.** Then I wanted to teach every level of students, and since then I have. I leaned how to get control of class behaviors at all costs.

Vary Approaches to Work With Challenged and Culturally Different Students

This teacher remained calm and consistent when working with a highly aggressive deaf student no matter what the student attempted to do. She always shaped his behavior, reinforced him, and gave him clear directions when he started to complain. I was amazed that she **stayed so calm** with this student, who is bigger than she and about to take her arm off if she upsets him (he loved to bite people). It taught me to always **respect the student and stay calm** or get out of the situation.

When I had difficulty maintaining control of a student with autism, another teacher demonstrated how to **use a carpet square to provide specific and clear boundaries to the students.** I began to think about how specific disabilities affect behavior, and it expanded my ideas to include methods related to specific disabilities.

I learned that I could **call a special education student's caseload teacher** to contact a student's parent rather than calling her myself every time the student behaved inappropriately.

My first response to a self-contained mainstream student was to discipline her when she could not control her language, but I observed a teacher who **overlooked her expected unacceptable behavior and who was able to quickly redirect the student.** Now I am able to **reframe situations** so I don't explode when a student erupts with a tirade, and I have less anger when students make outbursts.

A teacher taught me about **understanding the differences among cultures**—for example, that many African American students don't look adults in the eyes when being corrected, out of respect. Now I look beyond the surface and truly try to understand why our students behave as they do. I stop and think it through, and I don't make quick judgments. I am keenly aware of the very different backgrounds of my students.

SUMMARY

Throughout this chapter we presented a host of ways that peer consultants helped teachers improve classroom management. Specifically, we discussed peer consultation skill #5, guiding for classroom management, which spotlights nine effective guiding principles: matching academics to students needs, taking a love approach, insisting on student responsibility and natural consequences, remaining calm and quiet, not taking things personally, being consistent, considering students' goals related to misbe-havior, being proactive, and not overdoing it. The chapter closed with lessons teachers learned from peer consultants about setting up and main-taining classroom routines including beginning the year right; having plans and systems; using warm-ups, signals, and proximity; adjusting seat-ing; tracking behavior; experimenting with varied techniques; using body language; and using caring approaches when working with challenged and culturally different students. Chapter 7, Unleashing the Hidden Potential of Peer Consultation, discusses, among other things, major con-clusions drawn from our study, our concept of academic leadership, find-ings about the link between peer consultation and professional learning community, and suggestions for promoting peer consultation.

QUESTIONS FOR DISCUSSION AMONG FACULTY AND ADMINISTRATORS

1. Peer consultants in our study helped teachers by sharing nine guid-ing principles for classroom management. To what degree do fac-ulty members and administrators in your school agree on these principles? Do you need to adapt or revise any of the principles to make them reflect what should be done at your school?

2. Have teachers reflect on their first year of teaching and any valuable lessons they learned from peer consultants about setting up and maintaining classroom routines (see Figure 6.1). If these lessons have stood the test of time, are they being shared with novice teachers in your school?

3. In what ways and to what degree have teachers' *horror stories* affected their teaching? Could other teachers have helped when such negative events occurred? What does this say about collegial support and encouragement?

SUGGESTED READING FOR FURTHER LEARNING

Classroom Management

Cummings, C. (2000). *Winning strategies for classroom management.* Alexandria, VA: Association for Supervision and Curriculum Development.

Gordon, S. P., & Maxey, S. (2000). *How to help beginning teachers succeed.* Alexandria, VA: Association for Supervision and Curriculum Development.

Lee, C. (2004). *Preventing bullying in schools: A guide for teachers and other professionals.* Thousand Oaks, CA: Corwin Press.

Marzano, R. J., Marzano, J. S., & Pickering, D. J. (2003). *Classroom management that works: Research-based strategies for every teacher.* Alexandria, VA: Association for Supervision and Curriculum Development.

McLeod, J., Fisher, J., & Hoover, G. (2003). *The key elements of classroom management: Managing time and space, student behavior, and instructional strategies.* Alexandria, VA: Association for Supervision and Curriculum Development.

Stone, R. (2005). *Best classroom management practices for reaching all learners: What award-winning classroom teachers do.* Thousand Oaks, CA: Corwin Press.

Sullivan, K., Cleary, M., Sullivan, G. (2004). *Bullying in secondary schools: What it looks like and how to manage it.* Thousand Oaks, CA: Corwin Press.

Challenged and Culturally Different Students

Baldwin, A. Y. (Ed.). (2004). *Culturally diverse and underserved populations of gifted students.* Thousand Oaks, CA: Corwin Press.

Bender, W. N. (2002). *Differentiating instruction for students with learning disabilities: Best teaching practices for general and special educators.* Thousand Oaks, CA: Corwin Press.

Calderón, M. E., & Minaya-Rowe, L. (2003). *Designing and implementing two-way bilingual programs.* Thousand Oaks, CA: Corwin Press.

Lachat, M. A. (2004). *Standards-based instruction and assessment for English language learners.* Thousand Oaks, CA: Corwin Press.

McNary, S. J., Glasgow, N. A., & Hicks, C. D. (2005). *What successful teachers do in inclusive classrooms: 60 research-based teaching strategies that help special learners succeed.* Thousand Oaks, CA: Corwin Press.

Robins, K. N., Lindsey, R. B., Lindsey, D. B., & Terrell, R. D. (2002). *Culturally proficient instruction: A guide for people who teach.* Thousand Oaks, CA: Corwin Press.

Snow, D. R. (2005). *Classroom strategies for helping at-risk students.* Alexandria, VA: Association for Supervision and Curriculum Development.

Sousa, D. A. (2001). *How the special needs brain learns.* Thousand Oaks, CA: Corwin Press.

Villa, R. A., & Thousand, J. S. (2005). *Creating an inclusive school.* Alexandria, VA: Association for Supervision and Curriculum Development.

7

Unleashing the Hidden Potential of Peer Consultation

W e begin this chapter with a discussion of research relevant to peer consultation. Next, we identify some of the major conclusions about peer consultation supported by our findings and suggest that teachers, administrators, and staff developers construct actions consistent with such conclusions. Our concept of academic leadership, based on this and other research, is also introduced. A brief discussion of *catalysts for teacher growth* is followed by a detailed presentation of our findings about the link between peer consultation and the development of professional learning communities. We also discuss our findings about semiformal collaboration and its effects. This chapter closes with several recommendations for unleashing and sustaining peer consultation in school settings.

BACKGROUND

Twenty years have passed since Little (1985) observed interactive relationships between teacher advisers and teachers working together to improve instruction in Marin County, California. Little discovered a dilemma: On one hand, although teachers found conferences with advisers stimulating, rewarding, a boost to one's ego, and an opportunity they would eagerly repeat, they were still hesitant to approach an adviser. On the other hand, because advisers assumed entry to the teachers' world would be hard-won, they were ambivalent about *stepping on toes*; therefore, they resorted to recruiting interested individuals on a case-by-case basis. This approach produced pairs of teachers whose work was based on mutual respect and skillful, informal influence rather than bureaucratic authority. Little found that these pairs of educators modeled six facilitative and supportive technical principles of peer advising:

1. use of a common language;

2. focus on one or two key questions;

3. use of evidence from the record of classroom interaction;

4. lively interaction and joint problem solving;

5. trust building through reliance on a predictable set of topics, criteria, and methods; and

6. reciprocity through careful thought and attention as well as preservation of individual dignity.

These findings are similar to those of other research about the effects of teacher leadership on colleagues' classrooms and school-level practices, and as such, confirm that school cultures (e.g., those characterized by isolation, lack of inquiry, reluctance to interfere with others' work) can be a serious obstacle to achieving gains from peer collaboration (York-Barr & Duke, 2004).

In the past decade, studies of teachers' professional development have shifted to focus on the positive effects of relationships with colleagues (Floden, 2001), particularly with regard to teachers' perceptions of gains from participation in networks of teaching (Lieberman & McLaughlin, 1994). These studies point out that teachers learned to teach from one another; however, the effects of collaboration on student learning were not established. In contrast, in Chapters 1 through 6 of this book, we examined a form of peer consultation that occurred naturally and spontaneously and required no special training or official support. We also examined the effects of peer consultation on student learning as perceived by teachers involved in our study. We have seen that, in the teachers' view, naturally occurring collaboration expands teachers' repertoires of teaching and learning strategies, increases teachers' ability to meet diverse student needs, enhances teachers' confidence and self-esteem, and increases teachers' commitment to continuing professional growth and development. Peer consultants build healthy relationships with teachers by communicating, caring, and developing trust; exploiting the knowledge base; planning and organizing with teachers for learning; showing and demonstrating different kinds of lessons and sharing professional expertise and artifacts; and guiding teachers for classroom management. There is little doubt that the teachers who participated in our study valued the lessons they learned from their peer consultants. Small wonder! Who besides another teacher best understands the challenges and dynamics of a specific group of students? Who knows better about the potential pitfalls and mistakes common to teaching than another teacher?

CAPITALIZING ON THE POWER OF PEER CONSULTATION

To capitalize on the power of peer consultation, we recommend that all educators, especially teachers, administrators, and staff developers, consider supportive actions consistent with our findings:

- *Teachers should learn from each other.* According to our data, many of teachers' most helpful lessons (e.g., planning for teaching, motivating students, using technology for learning, engaging students, providing hands-on learning experiences for diverse students, and measuring learning) were provided by other teachers, their peer consultants.
- *Teachers should be models for each other.* Teachers reported that their peers provided positive teaching models to emulate; they also clarified why certain teacher behaviors had negative effects that were potentially damaging to students.
- *Teachers should share their motivation and inspiration with each other.* Peer consultants, our data point out, were a major source of innovation in the classroom; their conversations with teacher colleagues created a cross-fertilization of strategies, materials, and approaches that should become part of a school's ongoing professional development program (see Husby, 2005; Tate, 2004; and Wheelan, 2005 for seminal work on indispensable learning strategies for individual and group development).
- *Teachers should reflect, discuss, and debate instructional matters with their colleagues.* We propose that teachers become activists regarding teacher empowerment by administrators, which must include multiple opportunities to work collaboratively. Unfortunately, our data indicate that teachers who lack such opportunities are less likely to be successful and more likely to leave teaching.
- *Teachers should learn about cognition and learning from colleagues.* The teachers we studied reported that in their peer conversations they discovered that learning is complex and is essential to contextually adapt and integrate learning to meet diverse student needs.

- *Teachers should use their own classrooms and artifacts from their teaching* (e.g., plans, videotapes of lessons, student work samples) *as the context for learning from peers.* This is consistent with the findings of other researchers (Borko, 2004).
- *Teachers should help each other learn how to deal with students' behavior.* We found that peer teachers helped one another learn how to handle class management problems, including how to be clear, fair, consistent, and calm, as well as how to involve students in classroom decision making.

Peer consultation can also include shared professional development experiences such as reading pairs, forums for solving instructional problems, and peer observation and reflection; thus it can provide a base for what has been called "parallel leadership . . . a process whereby *teacher leaders and their principals* engage in collective action to build school capacity" (Crowther, Kaagan, Ferguson, & Haan, 2002, p. 38). Such collaborative work is characterized by *mutualism* (i.e., teachers and principals share trust and respect and are thereby interdependent in designing and implementing innovation); *a sense of shared purpose* by which the school's vision and approaches to teaching, learning, and assessment foster a positive school culture; and *mutual expression* (i.e., faculty can accommodate one another's values, thereby encouraging both individual expression and action as well as collaboration). *In parallel leadership, teachers assume primary leadership for improvement of teaching and learning, and principals assume primary leadership for aligning resources and facilitating alliances to support such improvements.*

AN ELEMENT OF ACADEMIC LEADERSHIP REVEALED

In other studies we have examined instructional leadership, teacher empowerment, the development of professional learning communities, and constructivist leading and learning in schools (e.g., Blase & Blase, 2001, 2004). We call the configuration of behaviors, attitudes, and skills associated with these phenomena, *academic leadership.* Academic leaders are educators who strive to participate fully in school improvement; develop a collaborative, democratic, trusting community of leader learners; and involve all others from the school community in participative, inquiry-oriented, constructivist decision making. The cornerstones of our model of academic leadership are

- the primacy of an instructional focus;
- the development of a culture of learning, analysis, and critique;
- participative decision making based on improvement of instruction; and
- development of viable group processes.

This broad-based model argues that effective academic leaders—both teachers and administrators—should emphasize teachers' professional growth and, in particular, reflection, to build a school culture of collaborative, data-based, critical examination among lifelong learners to improve teaching and learning. *We consider peer consultation to be an essential aspect of academic leadership and argue that opportunities for peer consultation be expanded within schools,* alongside existing formal programs such as teacher mentoring, teacher leadership, and teacher induction (all of which vary significantly in terms of effectiveness [Conley, Fauske, & Pounder, 2004; York-Barr & Duke, 2004]). Our model of academic leadership further argues that educators

- ensure that internal factors such as policies, norms, and teaching practices impact student and educator learning;
- sustain professional development, dialogue, inquiry, critique, and problem-solving approaches that drive school improvement; and
- enact leadership and teaching behaviors that theoretically and empirically demonstrate positive effects on learning.

TEACHERS TEACHING TEACHERS: PEER CONSULTANTS AT THEIR BEST

In Oja and Reiman's (1998) review of research on instructional supervision for teacher development, the authors recommended the application of developmental theory to the practice of supervision of teachers; we posit the relevance of such theory, not only to determine the conditions for promoting teacher growth and learning through formal supervision but also to promote peer consultation. The following four catalysts for teacher growth apply to peer consultation:

1. *Perturbation:* Teachers confront and reconcile *contradictions* to their preferred ways of teaching, gaps in their knowledge, and disturbances in their perspectives, which lead to more complex forms of thought and reflective abstraction (Piaget, 1985).

2. *Social Interaction:* Teachers perform at more advanced levels when *coaching and assistance* are *provided* (Vygotsky, 1978).

3. *Role-Taking:* Teachers who participate in *real world activities* (as opposed to role-playing or simulations of classroom activity) have greater potential for development (Mead, 1934).

4. *Reflection:* Teachers grow from the *interplay between action (experience) and reflection;* this is known as praxis (Dewey, 1933), reflection-in-action (Schön, 1987), or critical reflection (van Manen, 1977). Thus teachers at higher stages of reflection tend to be perceptive and

flexible in the classroom and constantly changing the learning environment with respect to student needs.

In addition, we suggest a fifth catalyst for peer consultation, based on our present study and the research of others such as Printy (2002) and Wenger (1998):

5. *Productive Participation in a Community of Practice:* Teachers fully participate in a community of practice to draw on the expertise of their colleagues; this is related to increased teacher learning, teacher competence, and teachers' use of standards-based pedagogy. Peer consultation, in particular, promotes teacher metacognition, which includes teachers' self-regulation, including changing teaching behavior to better suit the learning task, based on practice with feedback; monitoring, such as tracking behaviors during the performance of a teaching task; and volition, like invoking and controlling emotions and distractions (Bandura, 1986). Further, we note that peer consultants also demonstrate and grow in their metacognition abilities as they work with teachers.

HOW PEER CONSULTATION SUPPORTS THE DEVELOPMENT OF A PROFESSIONAL LEARNING COMMUNITY

In many ways, the ember of peer consultation ignites a flame to create a professional learning community among teachers. How does a tiny spark of conversation among peers lead to widespread collaboration in a school? Interestingly, *our data indicate that the development of peer consultative relationships among teachers frequently provoked further spontaneous development of informal professional learning communities; that is, pairs or groups of teachers in a school who organized in a variety of ways to observe, talk, reflect on, and improve their teaching.* The results of this (administratively unsanctioned) seemingly irresistible form of collaboration were dramatic for *pairs* of teachers and *groups* of teachers. Effects on the latter are illustrated in the following text:

Three to five of the department members eat lunch together and constantly share ideas, reflect on what is happening in classrooms, ask for help, and brainstorm situations.

I feel like I am part of a small community of teachers who are devoted to improving their practice. We have peer discussions; we bounce ideas off of each other and give feedback. It is really valuable in day-to-day workings of our classes. I am more reflective and I look more closely at what is happening. I have revised lessons and have improved my strategies, and I have become more confident in my abilities and more willing to change.

Several teachers decided to work together on science units with each teacher becoming an expert in one of the four areas. I was able to concentrate on one topic and always be on the lookout for supporting materials. Each time I presented my unit, I ended up making changes, fine-tuning the unit, and getting better student engagement as a result. It improved my use of time in the classroom. When I reflect on this experience, I find I enjoy having the time to fine-tune my craft. Teaching a lesson more than once is not boring like I thought it had to be; there is another reward. And any time one teacher spends time in another teacher's classroom, they can't help but pick up ideas from what they see and hear.

We went on a retreat and broke into groups in which we discussed different genres we were going to cover; we discussed our successes and failures. One teacher shared a particular strategy about group work which I was now willing to try. I went through the activity in my mind several times and tried to identify the pitfalls; it was a success in the classroom and now I am gearing my teaching toward more freedom for students. I have become more of a facilitator as a result and I realize that I have to prepare more to make activities successful. I enjoy this style of teaching as opposed to lecturing.

We constantly observe each other and reflect on and refine our teaching. I compared myself to my fellow teachers; I was able to think through what we did. My teaching improved because I incorporated the things the other teachers did well and balanced this with what the students in class did well. I enjoyed this work as a way to observe the strengths of others. Modeling by them allows me to sift through my thoughts and reflections.

All the teachers on my grade level shared activities they use in the reading program; now everyone has a variety of activities to use. We learned how to use reciprocal teaching by students in cooperative reading groups; this approach allows me as a teacher to work individually with students who really need me while students in the groups are getting what they need. I also use this strategy in math, social studies, and science. The students love being the teacher, and they work hard to do a good job at it; they also learn a lot from each other. It frees me to be where I need to be and it gives kids the responsibility for their own learning, it also controls small group behavior problems.

In essence, the teachers we studied revealed that group-oriented peer consultation, naturally embedded in their daily work, deepened the development of learning communities through critical reflection, improved classroom instruction, increased ability to self-evaluate, and increased work satisfaction and motivation. This was also true for *pairs* of teachers engaged in peer consultation:

> We observed each other's classes and then discussed ways to improve certain aspects of our classes. It improved my awareness of the environment in my classroom and my teaching improved in terms of student interest. I was scared at first that I was doing something wrong but now I am happy to have help.

> Planning and teaching jointly influences me because I know that I am meeting the needs of my students. It challenges me to come up with many ways to teach. It helps me modify, adapt, and play out in my mind what is best for the students. I get great satisfaction from team planning because I know we all have the same goals. It also makes our instruction richer.

> Ten years ago a peer teacher told me that "all children can learn." I had been very frustrated because I was teaching profound and severely disabled students. The severity of their disabilities was frustrating. This teacher began to model and make suggestions about how to feel good in this situation, and I finally did begin to feel successful. She shared information with me regarding her experiences with teaching situations similar to the ones that I was experiencing. She was a sounding board for problem solving and for talk about situations related to student behavior, learning, and parent relationships.

> The gifted resource teacher modeled for me an effective way to deliver the lesson. We took time to reflect, to discuss the planning, and to talk about the lessons and student reactions; it was invaluable for my own further planning and assessment; now I model my teaching after this approach, I feel relaxed and willing to try new things.

> She encouraged me to accept feedback from students. Now when I have to issue grades, I ask my students to grade me, to tell me one positive thing and one thing that I could do to improve my teaching.

SEMIFORMAL COLLABORATION AMONG TEACHERS AND ITS EFFECTS

In some cases, we found that groups of teachers who wanted to work together were able to secure modest amounts of *administrative support* for their collaborative work; significantly, such efforts grew out of teachers' natural inclination to collaborate with others. Said differently, teachers themselves lobbied administrators for resources, space, and more typically, time and opportunity to collaborate as a *team*. Excerpts from our database illustrate the impressive effects of minimal administrative support for teacher collaboration including increased reflection, attention to individual student needs, ability to integrate diverse subject matter, increased innovation and risk taking, development of expertise, efficient use of time, and generally *sharing the load:*

> We got the support of the administration to do some collaborative planning because we had earned the principal's trust through the years and our rationale was strong. It provides us with an opportunity to collaboratively make decisions and engage in reflective practice. We plan our own staff development to support our growth. This endeavor enables us to specialize in our content areas and to integrate our curriculum. We have a feeling of community among us, our students, and our parents.

> We debrief daily; we take about fifteen minutes and discuss activities that were motivating to our students and activities that were not motivating. We talk about changes that could be made to reach individual students, behavioral issues, and strategies to deal with certain lessons. It helps me to analyze daily actions between students and teachers and to direct my teaching to address individual needs. It gives me confidence in the classroom and a place to vent disturbing situations.

> We talk, problem solve about issues, and build stronger relationships. It helps me think a lot about my teaching, students, and issues. This dialogue allows me to reflect and problem solve. It affects the way I teach and interact with students. It changes my outlook on situations and topics. I feel better with a dialogue with other teachers because I can vent frustration and feel supported in the decisions I make.

> Together we had integrated our teaching in art, music, and physical education to incorporate our theme about problem solving; we are working with two professional artists, a dancer, and an actor to support the theme because we believe that art should be a part of children's learning processes. Now I work with these teachers to plan, organize, and teach this theme consistently. I feel it is a good program.

> We completed observation cycles and analyzed and reflected on our teaching and the impact of the instructional program on the lives of children in our care. I was able to fine-tune my instruction

and to plan and teach reflectively. I have increased my repertoire of teaching strategies, and I also feel supported and validated.

At the end of our team meetings, we give kudos to one another in order to positively recognize behaviors or events on the part of other staff members. Many comments are made and many teachers are recognized. It made me feel competent to know the specific actions others identified as impacting kids; I have tried to repeat those same behaviors so that students will continue to be successful, it made me feel proud of myself.

We were five physical education teachers who bonded immediately. We support each other by sharing new ideas, lesson plans, encouraging each other, and even providing constructive criticism. Constant feedback and unconditional support directly and indirectly helps us to become more effective teachers. If I have a bad day, they are there to pick me up and vice versa. One day when I was completely frustrated and unmotivated about a particular discipline incident with a child, one of the teachers helped me through it, making me realize that I had done the right thing. She also helped me think of a different way to work with the child next time. I feel supported, encouraged, able to take other points of view, challenged to create new ideas, enthusiastic, broadened in my ability to discover new approaches to lessons, more energetic as a teacher, and teaching is fun.

Further, within administratively sanctioned group efforts, teachers' natural tendency to *buddy up*—work together as peer consultants in *pairs* to improve instruction—was evident (and hardly surprising); that is, administrators' support of the *learning community* approach spontaneously spawned *peer consultation* embedded in learning communities of teachers just as (discussed previously) peer consultation was often the ember to ignite learning communities in schools:

My buddy and I switch off for daily reading with students. She showed me how to lead the students in a singing round while passing out materials; this is a great way to keep students on task and keep their attention, and my time is now used more effectively and I feel relieved because I am avoiding feelings of frustration.

I am influenced by my coteacher daily. We have shared many ideas; she is extremely interested in the teaching of writing, as I am, so we both read books on this topic and shared our ideas. It was a new type of writing for my students, and I was amazed at how much information they could gain using our new method. My students enjoyed working with this approach and type of information. We shared our expertise. As a group we read, talked, and processed a lot of information. We shared our expertise in informal chats and staff development sessions; we shared resources as well. This gave me new information and insight into my teaching; it provided me with new strategies so that I could rethink how I deliver reading. It inspired me to make changes in my teaching, and as a result my students' reading abilities have improved in time, quality, and breadth of choices.

I plan with my buddy for the social studies units, which drive the theme for the other integrated subjects. It is an enormous help because we make sure we cover and enrich our objectives. It encourages thinking for new ideas, and it is wonderful to be supported. We share information strategies, materials, pacing, and even help with completing paperwork daily. Our relationship has evolved into a friendly give and take with each of us knowing that we can rely on each other; it provides a strong network of support for teachers and it can make a huge difference in their success. Teaching is a demanding job, and knowing that you have others to talk to helps. We learn a lot from each other. If we teach together for many more years, I know our learning and sharing together will continue; we spur each other on. There is an element of friendly competition among us, and it does two things: it inspires us to put out renewed efforts sometimes when we need to push and it focuses us to do a complete and even better job with students. We enjoy sharing our students' successes as well.

I was fortunate to work with this team teacher, a veteran; many of the children we had were nonverbal. Her clear and simple directions, which were modeled along with her helping the children physically imitate actions which she demonstrated repeatedly, got the best of their verbal or nonverbal abilities. At the end of the year, they had increased language abilities, whether in comprehension or expression, so I have imitated her teaching, especially her questioning techniques. I feel more prepared and confident in teaching autistic, BD [behaviorally disordered], cerebral palsy populations. It made me realize that my experience as a teacher working with impaired children had prepared me for this needy population.

I respect my teammate tremendously; our philosophies of teaching and behavioral expectations mesh well together. I have grown as an educator by planning and teaching and evaluating together. We have tried new ideas and strategies because we had each other's support. It has been my best teaching experience. I have taken more risks in the classroom because I am not isolated.

I learned more from my colleague than I could from any professor or textbook. I observed her interactions and techniques daily. I also learned about classroom management, organization, and instructional techniques. It was the best experience because I could learn something, apply it, and receive feedback all in the same day. As a result, I found myself thinking about teaching in an entirely different light. I use more techniques than I had before. My colleague is a teacher before her time—she seems to be one step ahead of the trend. I still ask for her opinions and think about what she would do in similar situations.

We are constantly discussing the strategies we use to move children along in their reading. One teacher demonstrated the use of magnetic letters to help students see parts or chunks of words. She helped make it easier for me to make a shift in my own students' thinking and use of strategies for reading. She helped me see another way of helping the children. Now I use this method regularly. I realize that as we reflect on our teaching together, we sharpen each other's skills and we open ourselves up to be vulnerable; yet we gain approaches and new ideas. We practice every week our reading strategies in different life situations. I feel supported by this teacher and in this low-risk environment. I feel freer to think about strategies instead of trying to figure them out on my own. I learn more because I read about it, try it out, talk with others, and become able to critique myself making appropriate adjustments. It makes me highly motivated and it is a very positive experience.

CONCLUSION: THE CHALLENGE FOR TEACHERS, ADMINISTRATORS, AND PROFESSIONAL LEARNING COORDINATORS TO UNLEASH AND SUSTAIN PEER CONSULTATION

Clearly, the study results discussed throughout this book present a compelling example of organizational citizenship in teachers based on altruism, courtesy, conscientiousness, sportsmanship, and civic virtue; to wit, according to our data, peer consultants are teachers who "spontaneously [go] beyond formally prescribed job requirements and engage in nonmandatory behaviors without expectation of receiving explicit recognition or compensation" (Tschannen-Moran & Hoy, 2000, p. 583). We learned that this results in high levels of trust, communication, collaboration, and a spirit of professional community among teachers. Teachers themselves are the catalyst for building a learning community of open dialogue, inquiry, social justice, and caring. Because educators face an increasingly multicultural society with greater diversity and transience, cultivating teacher collaboration is paramount in education; teacher collaboration is at least one significant part of the path to greater teacher efficacy, satisfaction, commitment, and productivity. How can school educators manage collaborative work to support school improvement?

In his inquiry into six teachers' views on school change and culture, Raymond Horn (2000) demonstrated that conversation is a powerful tool in promoting educational change, and teacher empowerment is vital to starting that conversation. The point: Administrators, teachers, and professional learning coordinators should acknowledge that "the most reliable, useful, proximate, and professional help resides under the roof of the schoolhouse with the teaching staff itself" (Barth, 2001, p. 445). Thus all educators should

- diligently facilitate the opportunities and the conditions necessary for conversation, peer observation, and reflection among teachers;
- provide effective avenues of communication such as e-mail;
- empower pairs and groups of teachers, giving them authority to manage themselves (i.e., balance the group's need for decision-making authority with the school's need for coordination);
- make resources available;
- provide effective coordination; and
- provide appropriate professional development.

Our study underscores the fact that the valuable social capital teachers bring to their work is largely hidden and rarely exploited in constructive ways. Yet teachers, who work in the most human of enterprises, resist institutional limitations to true collegiality by subtly engaging one another in substantive, reflective dialogue in which they come to better understand themselves, their teaching, and student learning. Thus, developing teachers' ability to assist each other through peer consultation should be of paramount concern to today's educators; it is clearly a powerful path to professional development, efficacy, and school improvement. It is time to refrain from limiting teachers' opportunities for sustained reflection about what they do, it is time to vigorously foster teachers' critical intellectual traditions and independent judgment, and it is time to engage in a great conversation about the important, even universal questions of education.

SUGGESTED READING FOR FURTHER LEARNING

Professional Learning Communities

Crow, G. M., & Pounder, D. G. (2000). *Interdisciplinary teacher teams.* Alexandria, VA: Association for Supervision and Curriculum Development.

Martinez, M. C. (2004) *Teachers working together for school success.* Thousand Oaks, CA: Corwin Press.

Osterman, K. F., & Kottkamp, R. B. (2004). *Reflective practice for educators: Professional development to improve student learning.* Thousand Oaks, CA: Corwin Press.

Senge, P. M. (1990). *The fifth discipline: The art and practice of the learning organization.* Alexandria, VA: Association for Supervision and Curriculum Development.

Tichenor, M., & Heins, E. (2000). *Study groups: An inquiry-based approach to improving schools.* Alexandria, VA: Association for Supervision and Curriculum Development.

Wald, P. J., & Castleberry, M. S. (2000). *Educators as learners: Creating a professional learning community in your school.* Alexandria, VA: Association for Supervision and Curriculum Development.

Portfolios

Rolheiser, C., Bower, B., & Stevahn, L. (2000). *The portfolio organizer: Succeeding with portfolios in your classroom.* Alexandria, VA: Association for Supervision and Curriculum Development.

Wyatt, R. L., & Looper, S. (2004). *So you have to have a portfolio: A teacher's guide to preparation and presentation.* Thousand Oaks, CA: Corwin Press.

Resource: Research Methods and Procedures

This book focuses on skills and related actions that teachers reported directly or indirectly influenced their teaching in a positive manner, specifically the effects of such actions on teachers' reflection, instruction, and feelings: teachers' perspectives or naturally occurring teacher-to-teacher consultation.

Data collection and analysis were consistent with symbolic interaction theory. Although this approach acknowledges that structural factors influence human action, the meanings that people attribute to action are emphasized. In essence, people's reflexivity is given greater importance than structural factors. As a product of social action, the individual is influenced by others but also maintains sufficient distance from others and is capable of initiating individual action (Blumer, 1969; Mead, 1934). Symbolic interaction, in contrast to some qualitative research approaches, stresses individual perception and interpretation.

Consistent with exploratory-inductive approaches to qualitative inquiry, no a priori definitions of teachers' helping actions were used to direct data collection. Accordingly, for the study reported in this book, we used open-ended questions and investigated the broad question, What actions by other teachers have helped teachers teach more effectively? We gathered data and analyzed these data to produce descriptive categories, themes, and conceptual and theoretical understandings (Bogdan & Biklen, 1982; Bogdan & Taylor, 1975; Glaser, 1978; Glaser & Strauss, 1967; Taylor & Bogdan, 1998).

Allport (1942) has argued that an open-ended questionnaire is considered a personal document in qualitative research that examines a person's subjective perspectives. Such a questionnaire is defined as any "self-revealing document that intentionally or unintentionally yields information regarding the structure, dynamics, and functioning of the author's life"

(p. xii). A questionnaire is a personal document when research participants have substantial control over the content of their responses.

We designed the Inventory of Teacher Actions that Positively Influence Your Teaching (ITAPIYT), an open-ended questionnaire, to collect personal meanings about the study topic. An initial version of this inventory was developed in consultation with professors and teachers and pilot tested with 50 full-time teachers. The following instruction appeared on each page of the final version of the ITAPIYT:

> Describe in detail *one action* on each of the following pages (what another teacher did) that directly or indirectly helped you teach more effectively. Please give examples to clarify what you mean.

In addition, we asked teachers to describe the *exact effects* of the teacher's action identified previously on their thinking, teaching, and feelings. The survey included five pages with the same questions; thus a teacher had the opportunity to describe, in detail, up to five actions and their effects on thinking, teaching, and feelings. Given the open-ended nature of the inventory, a period of approximately 35 minutes was required for its completion. Participation in this study was voluntary, and all questionnaires were completed anonymously. The procedure generated more than 1,000 pages of data (i.e., more than 1,000 actions), all examples of peer teacher actions and their effects on teachers' thinking, feeling, and professional performance.

We administered the inventory to a total of 297 teachers taking graduate courses at one major state university located in the southeastern United States. The study sample consisted of female (78%) and male (22%) teachers from rural (19%), suburban (65%), and urban (16%) schools. Elementary (49%), middle (24%), and high school (27%) teachers participated. The average age of teachers was 37 years; the average number of years in teaching was 11. Married (78%), single (18%), and divorced (4%) teachers participated. Degrees earned were B.A. or B.S. (34%), M.Ed. (49%), Ed.S. (14%), and Ed.D./Ph.D. (3%).

The study sample is roughly consistent with the national distribution of teachers with respect to gender, number of years of teaching, school level, and marital status. A lower average age, lower percentage of teachers with bachelor's degrees, a higher percentage of teachers with master's or specialist's degrees, and a lower percentage of teachers from urban and rural regions and higher percentage from suburban regions were represented in the sample compared with the national distribution (National Education Association, 2003).

Two researchers coded data from the study respondents according to principles for inductive research and comparative analyses (Bogdan & Biklen, 1982; Glaser, 1978, 1998, Glaser & Strauss, 1967; Taylor & Bogdan, 1998). This form of analysis required a comparison of each new unit of data to those coded previously for emergent categories and subcategories. Display matrixes were used to identify and refine conceptual and theoretical ideas derived from the data. This protocol also permitted comparisons of the descriptive and theoretical ideas produced by the study with the relevant extant literature (Bogdan & Biklen, 1982; Fontana & Frey, 2000; Glaser, 1978, 1998; Glaser & Strauss, 1967; Taylor & Bogdan, 1998). Professors, doctoral students, and teachers were consulted when questions arose.

From analyses of our data of peer teachers' characteristics that positively influence teaching, we produced three major themes consisting of 14 categories:

> Theme 1: *Teacher–teacher discourse* such as spontaneity, commitment, and expertise
>
> Theme 2: *Teacher–teacher interaction* such as planning, development of theoretical and conceptual approaches, development of technical skills, and mutual growth
>
> Theme 3: *Outcomes* such as effects related to philosophy, collaboration, benefits to students, instructional improvement, personal and professional growth, individualization, and diversity as well as effects on teachers' thinking (e.g., reflection, inquiry orientation, questioning), and feelings (e.g., confidence, desire for growth and reduced anxiety)

For purposes of this book, findings are presented consistent with the knowledge base about professional teacher learning and student learning. This book, drawn directly from our study data, describes peer consultation actions and their effects on teachers and offers a number of conceptual ideas about the nature of teacher–teacher interaction, teachers' knowledge construction, and pedagogical learning. Given space limitations, direct quotations from our database are only used to illustrate select ideas.

References

Acheson, K. A., Shamsher, M., & Smith, N. S. (1998). Supervision and instructional development. In G. R. Firth & E. F. Pajak. (Eds.), *Handbook of research on school supervision* (pp. 763–781). New York: Simon & Schuster Macmillan.

Allport, G. (1942). *The use of personal documents in psychological science.* New York: Social Science Research Council.

Bandura, A. (1986). *Social foundations of thought and action: A social cognitive theory.* Englewood Cliffs, NJ: Prentice Hall.

Barth, R. S. (1990*). Improving schools from within: Teachers, parents, and principals can make the difference.* San Francisco: Jossey-Bass.

Barth, R. S. (2001). Teacher leader. *Phi Delta Kappan, 82,* 443–449.

Beane, J. A., & Brodhagen, B. L. (2001). Teaching in middle schools. In V. Richardson (Ed.), *Handbook of Research on Teaching* (4th ed., pp. 1157–1174). Washington, DC: American Educational Research Association.

Beck, L. G. (1994). *Reclaiming educational administration as a caring profession.* New York: Teachers College Press.

Blase, J. (1991). *The politics of life in schools: Power, conflict, and cooperation.* Newbury Park, CA: Corwin Press.

Blase, J., & Blase, J. (1997). *The fire is back! Principals sharing school governance.* Thousand Oaks, CA: Corwin Press.

Blase, J., & Blase, J. (1999). Principals' instructional leadership and teacher development: Teachers' perspectives. *Educational Administration Quarterly, 35,* 349–378.

Blase, J., & Blase, J. (2002). The micropolitics of instructional supervision: A call for research. *Educational Administration Quarterly, 38*(1), 6–44.

Blase, J., & Blase, J. (2004a). *Handbook of instructional leadership: How successful principals promote teaching and learning* (2nd ed.). Thousand Oaks, CA: Corwin Press.

Blase, J., & Blase, J. (2004b, November). *Naturally-occurring facilitation among teachers: Implications for school leadership.* Paper presented at the annual meeting of the University Council for Educational Administration, Kansas City, MO.

Blase, J., & Blase, J. R. (1994). *Empowering teachers: What successful principals do.* Thousand Oaks, CA: Corwin Press.

Blase, J., & Blase, J. R. (2001). *Empowering teachers: What successful principals do* (2nd ed.). Thousand Oaks, CA: Corwin Press.

Blase, J., Blase, J. R., Anderson, G., & Dungan, S. (1995). *Democratic principals in action: Eight pioneers.* Thousand Oaks, CA: Corwin Press.

Bloom, B. S. (1984). The 2 sigma problem: The search for methods of instruction as effective as one-to-one tutoring. *Educational Researcher, 13*(6), 4–16.

Blumer, H. (1969). *Symbolic interactionism: Perspective and method.* Englewood Cliffs, NJ: Prentice Hall.

Bogdan, R., & Taylor, S. (1975). *Introduction to qualitative research methods: A phenomenological approach to the social sciences.* New York: Wiley.

Bogdan, R. C., & Biklen, S. K. (1982). *Qualitative research for education: An introduction to theory and methods* (2nd ed.). Boston: Allyn & Bacon.

Borko, H. (2004). Professional development and teacher learning: Mapping the terrain. *Educational Researcher, 33*(8), 3–15.

Borko, H., & Putnam, R. (1996). Learning to teach. In D. C. Berliner & R. C. Calfee (Eds.), *Handbook of educational psychology* (pp. 673–708). New York: Macmillan.

Brazosport Independent School District (Producer). (2003). *Teaching to standards: The 8-step instructional cycle* [videotape]. Arlington, VA: Educational Research Service.

Brookover, W. B., Beady, C., Flood, P., Schweitzer, J., & Wisenbaker, J. (1979). *School social systems and student achievement: Schools can make a difference.* New York: Praeger.

Brown, J. J., & Duguid, P. (1991). Organizational learning and communities of practice: Toward a unified view of working, learning, and organization. *Organization Science, 2*(1), 40–50.

Bryk, A., & Schneider, B. (2002). *Trust in schools: A core resource for improvement.* New York: Russell Sage.

Burden, P. R. (1990). Teacher development. In W. R. Houston, M. Haberman & J. Sikula (Eds.), *Handbook of research on teacher education* (pp. 311–328). New York: Macmillan.

Byrne, B. M. (1994). Burnout: Testing for the validity, replication, and invariance of causal structure across elementary, intermediate, and secondary teachers. *American Educational Research Journal, 31*(Fall), 645–673.

Capper, C. A., Frattura, E., & Keyes, M. W. (2000). *Meeting the needs of students of all abilities.* Thousand Oaks, CA: Corwin Press.

Carnegie Foundation for the Advancement of Teaching. (1986). *A nation prepared: Teachers for the 21st century.* Report of the Task Force on Teaching as a Profession. New York: The Foundation.

Carter, K. (1990). Teachers' knowledge and learning to teach. In R. W. Houston (Ed.), *Handbook of research on teacher education* (pp. 291–310). New York: Macmillan.

Cawelti, G. (Ed.). (2004). *Handbook of research on improving student achievement.* Arlington, VA: Educational Research Service.

Conley, S., Fauske, J., & Pounder, D. G. (2004). Teacher work group effectiveness. *Educational Administration Quarterly, 40*(5), 663–703.

Corallo, C. (1995). Influences on the development of informal teacher leaders (Doctoral dissertation, Virginia Polytechnic Institute and State University, 1995). *Dissertation Abstracts International, 56* (12), 4618A.

Cotton, K. (1995). *Effective schooling practices: A research synthesis. 1995 update. School Improvement Research Series.* Portland, OR: Northwest Regional Educational Laboratory.

Creemers, B. P. M. (1994). *The effective classroom.* London: Cassell.

Crowther, F., Kaagen, S. S., Ferguson, M., & Haan, L. (2002). *Developing teacher leaders: How teacher leadership enhances school success.* Thousand Oaks, CA: Corwin Press.

Daft, R. L., & Weick, K. E. (1984). Toward a model of organizations as interpretation systems. *Academy of Management Journal, 9*(2), 287–295.

Darling-Hammond, L., Bullmaster, M. L., & Cobb, V. L. (1995). Rethinking teacher leadership through professional development schools. *The Elementary School Journal, 96,* 87–106.

Dewey, J. (1933). *How we think: A restatement of the relation of reflective thinking to the educative process.* Chicago: Henry Regnery.

DuFour, R., & Eaker, R. (1998). *Professional learning communities at work: Best practices for enhancing student achievement.* Alexandria, VA: Association for Supervision and Curriculum Development.

Edmonds, R. R. (1979). *A discussion of the literature and the issues related to effective schooling.* Cambridge, MA: Center for Urban Studies, Harvard Graduate School of Education.

Enomoto, E. K. (1997). Negotiating the ethics of care and justice. *Educational Administration Quarterly, 33*(3), 351–370.

Erikson, E. H. (1959). *Identity and the life cycle.* New York: International Universities Press.

Evertson, C. M., & Smithey, M. W. (2000). Mentoring effects on proteges' classroom practice: An experimental field study. *The Journal of Educational Research, 93*(5), 294–304.

Fenstermacher, G. D., & Richardson, V. (1993). The elicitation and reconstruction of practical arguments in teaching. *Journal of Curriculum Studies, 25,* 101–114.

Floden, R. E. (2001). Research on effects of teaching: A continuing model for research on teaching. In V. Richardson (Ed.), *Handbook of Research on Teaching* (pp. 3–16). Washington, DC: American Educational Research Association.

Fontana, A., & Frey, J. H. (2000). The interview: From structured questions to negotiated text. In N. Denzin & Y. Lincoln (Eds.), *Handbook of qualitative research* (2nd ed., pp. 645–672). Thousand Oaks, CA: Sage.

Fraser, B. J., Walberg, H. J., Welch, W. W., & Hattie, J. A. (1987). Synthesis of educational productivity research [Special issue]. *Journal of Educational Research, 11*(2).

Fullan, M. (2003). *The moral imperative of school leadership.* Thousand Oaks, CA: Corwin Press.

Fuller, F. F., & Brown, O. H. (1975). Becoming a teacher. In K. Ryan (Ed.), *Teacher education,* (74th yearbook of the National Society for the Study of Education, Part II, pp. 25–52). Chicago: University of Chicago Press.

Garmston, R. J. (1987). How administrators support peer coaching. *Educational Leadership, 44*(5), 18–27.

Glanz, J. (1995). Exploring supervision history: An invitation and agenda. *Journal of Curriculum and Supervision, 10*(2), 95–113.

Glaser, B. G. (1978). *Theoretical sensitivity: Advances in the methodology of grounded theory.* Mill Valley, CA: Sociology Press.

Glaser, B. G. (1998). *Doing grounded theory: Issues and discussions.* Mill Valley, CA: Sociology Press.

Glaser, B. G., & Strauss, A. L. (1967). *The discovery of grounded theory: Strategies for qualitative research.* Chicago: Aldine.

Glickman, C. D., Gordon, S. P., & Ross-Gordon, J. M. (1995). *Supervision of instruction: A developmental approach* (3rd ed.). Boston: Allyn & Bacon.

Glickman, C. D., Gordon, S. P., & Ross-Gordon, J. M. (2004). *Supervision and instructional leadership: A developmental approach* (5th ed.). Boston: Allyn & Bacon.

Goldsberry, L. F. (1998). Teacher involvement in supervision. In G. R. Firth & E. F. Pajak (Eds.), *Handbook of Research in School Supervision* (pp. 428–462). New York: Simon & Schuster Macmillan.

Gordon, S. P. (1997). Has the field of supervision evolved to a point that it should be called something else? In J. Glanz & R. F. Neville (Eds.), *Educational supervision: Perspectives, issues, and controversies* (pp. 114–123). Norwood, MA: Christopher-Gordon.

Gould, R. (1972). The phases of adult life: A study in developmental psychology. *American Journal of Psychiatry, 129*, 521–531.

Gregorc, A. (1979). Learning/teaching styles: Their nature and effects. In *Student learning styles: Diagnosing and prescribing programs* (pp.19–26). Reston, VA: National Association of Secondary School Principals.

Gregory, G. (2005). *Differentiating instruction with style: Aligning teacher and learner intelligences for maximum achievement.* Thousand Oaks, CA: Corwin Press.

Gregory, G. H., & Chapman, C. (2005). *Differentiating instructional strategies: One size doesn't fit all.* Thousand Oaks, CA: Corwin Press.

Green, R. L. (1998). Nurturing characteristics in schools related to discipline, attendance, and eighth grade proficiency test scores. *American Secondary Education, 26*(4), 7–14.

Grimmett, P. P., & MacKinnon, A. M. (1992). Craft knowledge and the education of teachers. *Review of Research in Education, 18*, 385–456.

Guskey, T., & Sparks, D. (1996, Fall). Exploring the relationship between staff development and improvements in student learning. *Journal of Staff Development, 17*(4), 4–37.

Guthrie, H. D., & Willower, D. J. (1973). The ceremonial congratulation: An analysis of principals' observational reports of classroom teaching. *High School Journal, 56*(6), 284–290.

Hargreaves, A. (1994). *Changing teachers, changing times: Teachers' work and culture in the postmodern age.* New York: Teachers College Press.

Hargreaves, A., & Dawe, R. (1990). Paths of professional development: Contrived collegiality, collaborative culture, and the case of peer coaching. *Teaching and Teacher Education, 6*(3), 227–241.

Hattie, J. (1992). Measuring the effects of schooling. *Australian Journal of Education, 36*(1), 5–13.

Heller, M. F., & Firestone, W. A. (1995). Who's in charge here? Sources of leadership for change in eight schools. *The Elementary School Journal, 96*, 65–85.

Holmes Group. (1986). *Tomorrow's teachers: A report of the Holmes Group.* East Lansing, MI: The Holmes Group.

Holt, A. (1992). *Colleague consultation, a self-evaluation: Putting down on paper thoughts that range through my head on a daily basis.* Unpublished manuscript, cited by L. F. Goldsberry, Teacher involvement in supervision. In G. R. Firth & E. F. Pajak (Eds.), *Handbook of Research in School Supervision* (pp. 428–462). New York: Simon & Schuster Macmillan.

Horn, R. A. (2000). *Teacher talk: A post-formal inquiry into educational change.* New York: P. Lang.

Howey, K. R. (1988). Why teacher leadership? *Journal of Teacher Education, 39*, 28–31.

Husby, V. (2005). *Individualizing professional development.* Thousand Oaks, CA: Corwin Press.

Joyce, B., & Showers, B. (2002). *Student achievement through staff development* (3rd ed.). Alexandria, VA: Association for Supervision and Curriculum Development.

Joyce, B., Weil, M., & Calhoun, E. (2000). *Models of teaching* (6th ed.). Needham Heights: Allyn & Bacon.

Katzenmeyer, M., & Moller, G. (2001). *Awakening the sleeping giant: Leadership development for teachers.* (2nd edition). Thousand Oaks, CA: Corwin Press.

Kauffman, J. M., & Hallahan, D. P. (2005). *Special Education: What It Is and Why We Need It.* Boston: Pearson Education.

Klitgaard, R. E., & Hall, G. R. (1975). Are there unusually effective schools? *Journal of Human Resources, 10*(1), 90–106.

Knowles, M. S. (1978). *The adult learner: A neglected species.* Houston, TX: Gulf.

Kohlberg, L. (1969). State and sequence: The cognitive developmental approach to socialization. In D. Croslin (Ed.), *Handbook of Socialization Theory and Research* (pp. 347–380). New York: Rand McNally.

Kohler, F. W., Crilley, K. M., Shearer, D. D., & Good, G. (1997). Effects of peer coaching on teacher and student outcomes. *Journal of Educational Research, 90*(4), 240–250.

Krajewski, R. (1996). Supervision 2015. *Wingspan, 11*(2), 15–17.

Kroath, F. (1990, September). *The role of the critical friend in the development of teacher expertise.* Paper presented at the International Symposium on Research on Effective and Responsible Teaching, Universite de Fribourg Suisse, Fribourg, Switzerland.

Lambert, L., Walker, D., Zimmerman, D. P., Cooper, J. E., Lambert, M. D., Gardner, M. E., et al. (1995). *The constructivist leader.* New York: Teachers College Press.

Lave, J., & Wenger, E. (1991). *Situated learning: Legitimate peripheral participation.* Cambridge, MA: Cambridge University Press.

Leinhardt, G. (1993). On teaching. In R. Glaser (Ed.), *Advances in instructional psychology, Vol. 4* (pp. 1–54). Hillsdale, NJ: Lawrence Erlbaum.

Leithwood, K., & Jantzi, D. (2000). Principal and teacher leadership effects: A replication. *School Leadership and Management, 20,* 415–434.

Lewis, C. Perry, R., & Murata, A. (April, 2003). *Lesson study and teachers' knowledge development.* Paper presented at the annual meeting of the American Education Research Association, Chicago.

Lieberman, A. (1992). Teacher leadership: What are we learning? In C. Livingston (Ed.), *Teachers as leaders: Evolving roles* (pp. 159–165). Washington, DC: National Education Association.

Lieberman, A. (1995). Practices that support teacher development: Transforming conceptions of professional learning. *Phi Delta Kappan 76*(8), 591–596.

Lieberman, A., & McLaughlin, M. W. (1994). Networks for educational change: Powerful and problematic. *Phi Delta Kappan, 63,* 673–677.

Lieberman, A., & Miller, J. (1999). *Teachers—Transforming their world and their work.* New York: Teachers College Press.

Lipsey, M. W., & Wilson, D. B. (1993). The efficacy of psychological, educational, and behavioral treatment. *American Psychologist, 48*(12), 1181–1209.

Little, J. W. (1981). *School success and staff development: The role of staff development in urban desegregated schools. Executive summary.* Washington, DC: National Institute of Education.

Little, J. W. (1982). Norms of collegiality and experimentation: Workplace conditions of school success. *American Educational Research Journal, 19*(3), 325–340.

Little, J. W. (1985). Teachers as teacher advisors: The delicacy of collegial leadership. *Educational Leadership, 85*(43), 34–36.

Martin-Kniep, G. O. (2004). *Developing learning communities through teacher expertise.* Thousand Oaks, CA: Corwin Press.

Marzano, R. J. (1998). *A theory-based meta-analysis of research on instruction.* Aurora, CO: Mid-continent Research for Education and Learning.

Marzano, R. J. (2000). *A new era of school reform: Going where the research takes us.* Aurora, CO: Mid-continent Research for Education and Learning.

Marzano, R. J., Gaddy, B. B., & Dean, C. (2000). *What works in classroom instruction.* Aurora, CO: Mid-continent Research for Education and Learning.

Marzano, R. J., Norford, J. S., Paynter, D. E., Pickering, D. J., & Gaddy, B. B. (2001). *A handbook for classroom instruction that works.* Alexandria, VA: Association for Supervision and Curriculum Development.

Marzano, R. J., Pickering, D. J., & Pollock, J. E. (2001). *Classroom instruction that works: Research-based strategies for increasing student achievement.* Alexandria, VA: Association for Supervision and Curriculum Development.

Mayeroff, M. (1971). *On caring.* New York: Harper & Row.

McBride, M., & Skau, K. G. (1995). Trust, empowerment, and reflection: Essentials of supervision. *Journal of Curriculum and supervision, 10*(3), 262–277.

Mead, G. H. (1934). *Mind, self, and society.* Chicago: University of Chicago Press.

Miller, L. (1992). Teacher leadership in a renewing school. In C. Livingston (Ed.), *Teachers as leaders: Evolving roles* (pp. 115–129). Washington, DC: National Education Association.

Mortimore, P., Sammons, P., Stoll, L., Lewis, D., & Ecob, R. (1988). School matters. Berkley, CA: University of California Press.

Munby, H., Russell, T., & Martin, A. K. (2001). Teachers' knowledge and how it develops. In V. Richardson (Ed.), *Handbook of Research on Teaching* (pp. 877–904). Washington, DC: American Educational Research Association.

National Education Association (2003). Status of the American public school teacher. Washington, DC: National Education Association.

National Governors' Association. (1986). *Time for results.* Washington, DC: Author.

National Staff Development Council. (2001). *Standards for staff development* (Rev. ed.). Oxford, OH: Author.

Noddings, N. (1992). *The challenge to care in schools: An alternative approach to education.* New York: Teachers College Press.

Nonaka, I. (1994). A dynamic theory of organizational knowledge creation. *Organization Science, 5*(1), 14–37.

Odell, S. J. (1997). Preparing teachers for teacher leadership. *Action in Teacher Education, 19,* 120–124.

Oja, S. N., & Reiman, A. J. (1998). Supervision for teacher development across the career span. In G. R. Firth & E. F. Pajak (Eds.), *Handbook of research on school supervision* (pp. 463–492). New York: Simon & Schuster Macmillan.

Pajak, E. (1993). *Approaches to clinical supervision: Alternatives for improving instruction.* Norwood, MA: Christopher-Gordon.

Pellicer, L. O. (2003). *Caring enough to lead: Schools and the sacred trust.* Thousand Oaks, CA: Corwin Press.

Pellicer, L. O., & Anderson, L. W. (1995). *A handbook for teacher leaders.* Thousand Oaks, CA: Corwin Press.

Phillips, D. Y. (2004). *The perspectives of a principal and emergent teacher leaders of instructional leadership in a shared governance elementary school.* Unpublished doctoral dissertation, University of Georgia, Athens, GA.

Piaget, J. (1963). *Psychology of intelligence.* Totowa, NJ: Littlefield, Adams.

Piaget, J. (1985). *The equilibrium of cognitive structures.* Chicago: University of Chicago Press.

Poole, W. (1995). Reconstructing the teacher-administrator relationship to achieve systemic change. *Journal of School Leadership, 5*(6), 565–596.

Prawat, R. S. (1991). Conversations with self and settings: A framework for thinking about teacher empowerment. *American Educational Research Journal, 28*(4), 737–757.

Printy, S. M. (2002). *Communities of practice: Participation patterns and professional impact for high school mathematics and science teachers.* Unpublished dissertation. Columbus: The Ohio State University.

Pugach, M. C. (1990, April). *Self-study: The genesis of reflection in novice teachers?* Paper presented at the annual meeting of the American Educational Research Association, Boston.

Reitzug, U. C. (1994). A case study of empowering principal behavior. *American Educational Research Journal, 31* (2), 283–307.

Reitzug, U. C. (1997). Images of principal instructional leadership: From supervision to collaborative inquiry. *Journal of Curriculum Supervision, 12*(4), 324–343.

Reynolds, M. C., Wang, M. C., & Walberg, H. J. (1992). The knowledge base for special and general education. *Remedial and Special Education, 13*(5), 6–10.

Rosenholtz, S. (1985). Effective schools: Interpreting the evidence. *American Journal of Education, 93*(3), 349–355.

Rowan, B., Chiang, F. S., & Miller, R. (1997). Using research on employees' performance to study the effects of teachers on student achievement. *Sociology of Education, 70,* 256–284.

Rutter, M., Maughan, B., Mortimer, P., & Ouston, J. (1979). *Fifteen thousand hours: Secondary schools and their effects on children.* London: Open Books.

Sabatini, E. M. (2002). Teachers' perspectives of emergent teacher leadership in an elementary school (Doctoral dissertation, University of Georgia, 2002). *Dissertation Abstracts International-A, 63*(11), 3809.

Scheerens, J., & Bosker, R. J. (1997). *The foundations of educational effectiveness.* New York: Elsevier.

Schmuck, R. A., & Runkel, P. J. (1994). *The handbook of organizational development in schools and colleges* (4th ed.). Prospect Heights, IL: Waveland Press.

Schön, D. (1987). *Educating the reflective practitioner.* San Francisco: Jossey-Bass.

Schön, D. A. (1988). Coaching reflective teaching. In P. P. Grimmett & G. F. Erickson (Eds.), *Reflection in teacher education* (pp. 19–30). New York: Teachers College Press.

Schwab, R. L., & Foa, L .J. (2001). *Phi Delta Kappan, 82*(8), 620–625.

Sergiovanni, T. J. (1992). Moral authority and the regeneration of supervision. In C. D. Glickman (Ed.), *Supervision in transition: The 1992 ASCD Yearbook* (pp. 203–214). Reston, VA: Association for Supervision and Curriculum Development.

Shellard, E. (2003). *Using professional learning communities to support teaching and learning.* Arlington, VA: Educational Research Service.

Smylie, M. A. (1995). New perspectives on teacher leadership. *The Elementary School Journal, 96,* 3–7.

Smylie, M. A., & Brownlee-Conyers, J. (1992). Teacher leaders and their principals: Exploring the development of new working relationships. *Educational Administration Quarterly, 28,* 150–184.

Smylie, M. A., & Denny, J. W. (1990). Teacher leadership: Tensions and ambiguities in organizational perspective. *Educational Administration Quarterly, 26,* 235–259.

Smylie, M. A., & Hart, A. W. (1999). School leadership for teacher learning and change: A human and social capital development perspective. In J. Murphy & K. S. Louis (Eds.), *Handbook of research on educational administration* (2nd ed., pp. 421–441). San Francisco: Jossey-Bass.

Smyth, J. (1997). Is supervision more than the surveillance of instruction? In J. Glanz & R. F. Neville (Eds.), *Educational supervision: Perspectives, issues, and controversies* (pp. 286–295). Norwood, MA: Christopher-Gordon.

Sprinthall, N. A., & Thies-Sprinthall, L. (1980). Adult development and leadership training for mainstream education. In D. C. Corrigan & K. R. Howey (Eds.), *Concepts to guide the education of experienced teachers.* Reston, VA: Council for Exceptional Children.

Stigler, J. W., & Hiebert, J. (1999). *The teaching gap.* New York: Free Press.

Stone, M., Horejs, J., & Lomas, A. (1997). Commonalities and differences in teacher leadership at the elementary, middle, and high school levels. *Action in Teacher Education, 19,* 49–64.

Stroot, S. A., Fowlkes, J., Langholz, J., Paxton, S., Stedman, P., Steffes, L., et al. (1999). Impact of a collaborative peer assistance and review model on entry-year teachers in a large urban school setting. *Journal of Teacher Education, 50*(1), 27–41.

Sullivan, S., & Glanz, J. (2004). *Supervision that improves teaching: Strategies and techniques* (2nd ed.). Thousand Oaks, CA: Corwin Press.

Tate, M. L. (2004). *"Sit and get" won't grow dendrites.* Thousand Oaks, CA: Corwin Press.

Taylor, S. J., & Bogdan, R. (1998). *Introduction to qualitative research methods: A guidebook and resource* (3rd ed.). New York: Wiley.

Teitel, L. (1997). Professional development schools and the transformation of teacher leadership. *Teacher Education Quarterly, 24,* 9–22.

Tharp, R. G., & Gallimore, R. (1988). *Rousing minds to life.* New York: Cambridge University Press.

Tom, A. R., & Valli, L. (1990). Professional knowledge for teaching. In W. Houston (Ed.), *Handbook of research on teacher education* (pp. 373–392). New York: Macmillan.

Trachtman, R. (1991). Voices of empowerment: Teachers talk about leadership. In S. C. Conley & B. S. Cooper (Eds.), *The school as a work environment: Implications for reform.* Boston: Allyn & Bacon.

Tschannen-Moran, M., & Hoy, W. K. (2000). A multidisciplinary analysis of the nature, meaning, and measurement of trust. *Review of Educational Research, 70*(4), 547–593.

Van Manen, M. (1977). Linking ways of knowing with ways of being practical. *Curriculum Inquiry, 6,* 205–228.

Vygotsky, L. (1978). *Mind in society.* Cambridge, MA: Harvard University Press.

Wade, R. K. (1985). What makes a difference in inservice teacher education? A meta-analysis of research. *Educational Leadership, 42*(4), 48–54.

Walberg, H. J. (1980). *A psychological theory of educational productivity.* Washington, DC: National Institute of Education. (ERIC Document Reproduction Service No. ED 206 042)

Walberg, H. J., & Haertel, G. D. (Eds.) (1997). *Psychology and educational practice.* Berkley, CA: McCutchan.

Wang, M. C., Haertel, G. D., & Walberg, H. J. (1990). What influences learning? A content analysis of review literature. *Journal of Educational Research, 84,* 30–43.

Wang, M. C., Haertel, G. D., & Walberg, H. J. (1993). Toward a knowledge base for school learning. *Review of Educational Research, 63*(3), 249–294.

Wang, M. C., & Odell, S. J. (2002). Mentored learning to teach according to a standards-based reform: A critical review. *Review of Educational Research, 72,* 481–546.

Wasley, P. A. (1991). *Teachers who lead: The rhetoric of reform and the realities of practice.* New York: Teachers College Press.

Wenger, E. (1998). *Communities of practice: Learning, meaning, and identity.* New York: Cambridge University Press.

Wheelan, S. A. (2005). *Faculty groups: From frustration to collaboration.* Thousand Oaks, CA: Corwin Press.

York-Barr, J., & Duke, K. (2004). What do we know about teacher leadership? Findings from two decades of scholarship. *Review of Educational Research, 74*(3), 255–316.

Index

CORWIN PRESS

The Corwin Press logo—a raven striding across an open book—represents the union of courage and learning. Corwin Press is committed to improving education for all learners by publishing books and other professional development resources for those serving the field of PreK–12 education. By providing practical, hands-on materials, Corwin Press continues to carry out the promise of its motto: **"Helping Educators Do Their Work Better."**